D1433497

TEMPTING TREATS

Oriental

Party Food

For my Father and Mother

ACKNOWLEDGEMENTS

I am grateful to Antonia for her constant support and contribution; to my mother for her tenacity when typing up this manuscript; to Joanna and Muffy for their patience and to Alan and Ken for making photography an altogether pleasant experience.

TEMPTING TREATS

Oriental

Party Food

Paul Bloomfield

OVER 100 FESTIVE FOOD IDEAS

Macdonald Orbis

A Macdonald Orbis BOOK
© Macdonald & Co (Publishers) Ltd 1989

First published in Great Britain in 1989
by Macdonald & Co (Publishers) Ltd
London & Sydney
A member of Maxwell Pergamon Publishing Corporation plc

British Library Cataloguing in Publication Data
Bloomfield, Paul
    Tempting treats: Oriental party food
    1. Food: Asian party dishes — recipes
    I. Title
    641.5'68

ISBN 0-356-17963-X

Typeset by Bookworm Typesetting, Manchester
Printed and bound in Spain by Imprenta Hispano Americana S.A.

Senior Commissioning Editor: Joanna Lorenz
Art Editor: Muffy Dodson
Art Director: Linda Cole
Designer: Ingrid Mason
Photographer: Alan Newnham

Macdonald & Co (Publishers) Ltd
Headway House
66–73 Shoe Lane
London EC4P 4AB

CONTENTS

INTRODUCTION

The cuisines of the Far East, in particular China, Japan and Indonesia, all specialize in tiny items of food that are served as snacks, as part of a larger meal, or at street stalls. Many such as dimsum, sushi, spring rolls and spare ribs are now well known in the West and extremely popular. The recipes in this book have been chosen for their suitability as party food, for visual variety and for taste. They are authentic, although I am not a 'classic' cook and have written them so that they are easy to make in a Western kitchen.

Certain features make oriental food distinctive – one is the common core of ingredients such as garlic, ginger, spring onion and light and dark soy; another is the techniques of marinating and stir-frying. Marinating is important as it enhances the intrinsic flavours of the ingredients, and rapid stir-frying maintains the texture of the constituent parts of each dish. The procedure of cutting and chopping, then marinating, then last-minute stir-frying, is common to many of the recipes in this book.

Quantities
Plan your selection and preparation beforehand, bearing in mind that some recipes are more time-consuming than others. I would suggest at first choosing just 4–5 items for a party, allowing about 2–3 of

each per guest. Each recipe gives a guide to how many items it will make. For a larger party of say 40–60 people you should choose about 8 items to offer your guests for variety.

Shopping

Most of the ingredients in these recipes are now sold in the major supermarkets; they can also be found in health food shops, delicatessens and oriental shops. The bottled sauces such as soy and chilli, and items such as ginger, garlic and spring onion, are now quite common. You will need to go to an oriental supermarket for more esoteric items such as dried jellyfish, dumpling wrappers or guoba rice, but gradually you will find that you build up a stock of items that enables you to prepare from this book easily.

Equipment

Very little specialist equipment is required for oriental cooking, and improvisation is possible without affecting the quality of the food. However, if you do plan to do a lot of Far Eastern cooking, a few items will make your job a lot easier.

I use a wok for nearly all the cooking, whether stir-frying, deep-frying or steaming. Buy a flat-bottomed wok if you only have an electric hob, and make sure that you always use a round-bottomed wok with its stand, especially when frying.

Bamboo steamers are very cheap and useful as they can be stacked in layers for multiple steaming. Otherwise, normal metal steamers or a colander placed over a pan of boiling water work well. A bamboo rolling mat for preparing sushi is another good item, although you could use a linen cloth if absolutely necessary.

For the party, have to hand a variety of cocktail sticks, toothpicks and bamboo skewers for serving, and a number of small bowls for presenting the dipping sauces. Provide finger bowls and napkins if wished.

Planning and preparation

Pre-preparation is essential if you want to spend your party with your guests rather than in the kitchen. Nearly all the recipes in this book can be prepared beforehand to some extent. Deep-frying, however, is best done just before serving – items can be fried and then kept warm, but the flavour is even better if fried freshly.

Some items can be made in bulk and frozen so that all you need to do is bring them out and warm them through as and when required. It is a good idea to freeze basic items such as mandarin pancakes in small batches for easy removal, and also spring rolls, wontons and other dumplings.

Suggested menu of 8 items, with countdown

Choose a selection of items that include some cold items, some warm ones and 1–2 deep-fried ones. A good mixture would be vegetarian spring rolls (p.106), vegetable tempura (p.108), phoenix prawns (p.38), rice sushi (p.130), hoisin chicken [p.61], dried pepper beef (p.84), braised chinese mushrooms (p.116) and pork and shrimp wontons (p.80).

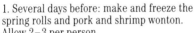

1. Several days before: make and freeze the spring rolls and pork and shrimp wonton. Allow 2–3 per person.

2. Day before: make sushi rolls, cover with cling film to prevent nori cracking and refrigerate. Prepare dry pepper beef and soak dried mushrooms overnight.

3. Morning before: shell and devein prawns and place in marinade. Prepare chicken and place in marinade. Remove spring rolls and wonton from freezer and leave to defrost, covered well so pastry does not dry out.

4. 2–3 hours before: prepare garnish for all items and cover until ready to use. Steam wontons and leave to cool, covered. Braise mushrooms and skewer dry beef with red pepper pieces. Lay out beef and mushrooms and cover. Remove sushi rolls from refrigerator, slice, lay in rows on a platter and cling film. Prepare tempura vegetables.

5. 30 minutes before: prepare tempura batter and garnish cold food.

6. During party deep-fry vegetable rolls for 2–3 minutes; stir-fry hoisin chicken; batter and deep-fry the tempura; steam wontons for a few minutes to reheat them and deep-fry phoenix prawns.

7. Have fun and enjoy your party!

Fish & Seafood

A mouthwatering catch of food from
the waters for you to try.

Fish and shellfish are classic ingredients in oriental party food, and are always extremely popular. There is a wide selection of items to choose from in this chapter, ranging from delicious deep-fried pieces such as crispy crab claws and sesame prawn toasts to raw fish sashimi.

I have mentioned already in the main introduction that many ingredients in this book can be found, cheaply, in oriental supermarkets. This is particularly true for fish and shellfish, and most Chinese shops stock a wide range in a selection of sizes and at a variety of prices. Many ingredients can be bought fresh or frozen, and it is easy to find raw prawns and shrimps in these stores. White fish however is often better bought at your local fishmonger, as it is then likelier to be in a more prepared state and easier to use. Economical white fish can be used.

Be cautious about preparing fish items too far in advance of your party: other sections such as meat and vegetables are more suitable for pre-cooking. Naturally many of the fish preparations can be carried out beforehand, such as the shelling and deveining of prawns, but the food will taste at its best if cooked just before serving.

Keep the garnishes as simple as possible – you certainly do not need elaborate garnishes for hot food; in fact I think the simpler the decoration generally the better. This maxim applies to most oriental food – which makes your job as host a lot easier!

NOODLE-WRAPPED PRAWNS

Makes 20

20 medium raw
  prawns, thawed if
  frozen, peeled,
  deveined, with tails
  intact
1 tsp salt

1 tbsp cornflour
1 egg yolk, lightly
  beaten
1 oz (25g) thin wonton
  noodles
1 sheet nori
vegetable oil for deep-
  frying

Make a shallow slit on underside of each
prawn so they can be straightened.
Sprinkle with salt and lightly dust with
cornflour, then dip into egg yolk. Break
noodles into pieces, lay on a plate and roll
each prawn over them. Cut nori into very
thin strips about 4" (10cm) long. Wrap a
strip a few times around each prawn and seal
with a little of the egg yolk.

Heat oil in a wok to 180°C/350°F, drop in
prawn bundles and deep-fry for 1½–2
minutes. Drain on kitchen paper and serve
warm.

SESAME PRAWN TOASTS

Makes 28

1 lb (450g) medium raw
  prawns, thawed if
  frozen
3/4 tsp salt
2 tsp cornflour
1 egg white, beaten
2oz (50g) pork fat,
  minced
8 water chestnuts
7 slices white bread,
  crusts removed
4oz (100g) white
  sesame seeds
vegetable oil for deep-
  frying

Peel and devein prawns: peel, cut a 1/4"
(5mm) deep slash along back of prawns
and remove black veins. Pull off heads. Pat
dry with kitchen paper and mince in a food
processor. Transfer to a bowl, add salt,
cornflour and egg white, and stir vigorously
for 2 minutes. Add pork fat and water
chestnuts and mix thoroughly. Refrigerate
for 1/2 hour.

Spread paste onto bread slices. Spread
sesame seeds on a dish and press slices
paste-side down to coat.

Half-fill a wok with oil and heat to
180°C/350°F. Fry paste-side down for 1 1/2
minutes, then turn over and fry until bread is
golden brown. Remove and drain on kitchen
paper. Cut each slice into 4 strips and serve.

SHRIMP AND CABBAGE DUMPLINGS

Makes 30

4 floz (110ml) water
14oz (425g) plain flour
14oz (425g) chinese
  cabbage
1 tsp salt
4oz (100g) dried
  shrimps, soaked in
  boiling water for 20
  minutes and drained
1 tsp shaosing wine or
  dry sherry
4 spring onions, finely
  chopped
hot chilli oil for dipping
light soy for dipping

Prepare dough: gradually add water to flour in a bowl and knead for 2 minutes. The dough should be firm. Cover and leave for ½ hour. Meanwhile shred cabbage, mix in a bowl with salt and also leave for ½ hour.

Chop shrimps finely; place in a bowl and mix with wine. Squeeze out excess water from cabbage and mix with shrimps and spring onions.

On a lightly floured surface roll dough into a long ¾" (2cm) cylinder. Cut into 30 × ¾" (2cm) slices. Roll out each piece to a 3" (7.5cm) circle. Place 1½ tsp filling in the centre of each wrapper, fold over and pinch to seal.

Poach dumplings in a pan of simmering water for 10 minutes, taking care they do not stick together. They will float to the surface when ready. Serve warm with bowls of hot chilli oil and soy for dipping.

SPICY SHRIMP NESTS

Makes 15

2oz (50g) dried wonton
  noodles
½ tbsp lightly beaten
  egg white
vegetable oil for deep-
  frying
4oz (100g) raw peeled
  shrimps, thawed if
  frozen

4 spring onions, white
  and green parts
  separated, cut into
  ½" (1cm) pieces
1 tsp cornflour
1 tbsp shaosing wine or
  dry sherry
2 tbsp chopped
  coriander
¼ tsp sweet chilli sauce
coriander for garnish

Take about 8 noodle strands and loosely
arrange in a small wire strainer, allowing
them to take their own shape, then dampen
with a little egg white using a pastry brush.
Half-fill a frying pan with oil and heat to
180°C/350°F. Take another similar-sized
strainer and press it lightly into the nest.
Hold the two together and place into hot oil.
Cook for about 30 seconds. Drain on kitchen
paper and repeat the process to make 15
nests.

To make the filling, sauté the shrimps
and spring onions in 1 tbsp oil in a pan, stir
in cornflour, splash in wine and stir well. Add
coriander and chilli sauce.

Scoop small amounts of filling into each
nest, garnish with coriander and serve cold.

CRAB TOASTS

Makes 40

8oz (225g) crabmeat,
  thawed if frozen
12oz (350g) raw
  peeled shrimps,
  thawed if frozen
2 tbsp cornflour
6–8 canned water
  chestnuts, finely
  chopped
10 large slices stale
  white bread, crusts
  removed

3 tbsp sesame seeds
corn oil for deep-frying
spring onion strips for
  garnish

SEASONINGS
2 tsp minced fresh
  ginger
1 tbsp rice wine vinegar
1 tsp salt
1 egg white, lightly
  beaten
1½ tsp sesame oil

U sing your fingers or a fork, shred
  crabmeat into small pieces. In a food
processor, process shrimps to a coarse paste.
Add all seasonings and process to a fine
paste. Transfer mixture to a bowl and add
cornflour, crabmeat and water chestnuts,
beating vigorously to a stiff paste.

Spread mixture thickly on bread slices,
using a spatula dipped in water to smooth
the paste. Sprinkle sesame seeds over the
top and press on lightly. With a sharp knife,
cut each slice into quarters diagonally.

Heat oil in a wok to 180°C/350°F. Add 6 or
7 crabmeat triangles at a time and deep-fry,
turning constantly until golden brown. Drain.
Repeat and serve hot, garnished with spring
onion.

FRAGRANT FISH

Makes 24

1½lb (700g) monkfish,
  cod or other firm
  white fish
1½ tbsp chopped
  spring onion
1 tbsp dark soy
white pepper
2 tbsp plain flour
corn oil for deep-frying

SAUCE

1½ tbsp dark soy
1½ tbsp malt vinegar
1½ tbsp shaosing wine
  or dry sherry
2½ tbsp sugar
¼–½ tsp 5-spice
  powder
1½ tbsp water

Skin fish, pat dry with kitchen paper and cut into about 24 pieces, 3 × 2" (7.5 × 5cm). Mix spring onion, soy and pepper in a bowl and stir in fish pieces to cover. Dust fish with flour using a sieve.

Half-fill a wok with oil and heat to 200°C/400°F and deep-fry fish pieces for 7–8 minutes until firm and brown at the edges. Remove, drain on kitchen paper and set aside.

Heat all sauce ingredients in a pan. Cook until sauce has reduced by one third, about 8–10 minutes; remove from heat, add fish and coat with sauce. Leave to cool before serving in a bowl accompanied by cocktail sticks.

CRISPY CRAB CLAWS

Makes 15

2oz (50g) pork fat, very
    finely diced
1 egg white
½ tsp cornflour
¼ tsp salt
¼–½ tsp white pepper
1 tsp caster sugar
1½ tsp water
9oz (250g) raw peeled
    shrimps, thawed if
    frozen
15 medium crab claws
2 eggs, beaten
½ large white stale
    loaf, crumbed
corn oil for deep-frying

Purée pork fat and egg white in a food
processor. Mix in cornflour, salt, pepper,
sugar and water. Add shrimps and process
mixture to a paste.

Dry crab claws with kitchen paper. Cover
each claw with shrimp mixture, making sure
it is pressed into place, but leaving the claw
exposed. Dip each claw into beaten egg, then
roll in breadcrumbs until the surface is
covered.

Half-fill a wok with oil and heat to
150°C/300°F and deep-fry claws for 2 minutes
until they are golden brown all over. Drain
on kitchen paper and serve hot.

HALIBUT PARCELS

Makes 50

*1 1/2lb (675g) halibut
   steaks
1/4pt (150ml) olive oil
1–1 1/2" (2.5–3.5cm)
   piece fresh ginger,
   peeled and finely
   shredded
10 large spring onions,
   cut into 1" (2.5cm)
   pieces and finely
   shredded
3 tbsp light soy
2 tbsp sesame oil
black or white pepper
2 heads iceberg lettuce*

R inse halibut and pat dry with kitchen paper. Place in a steamer. Steam, covered, over a pan of boiling water for about 10–15 minutes – the flesh should come away from the bones easily. Remove flesh, discarding bones, skin and liquid.

Heat a wok over high heat until smoke rises. Pour in olive oil, swirl it around, add ginger and spring onions and stir to release the aroma. Add fish, and turn and toss for 2–3 minutes; the fish will disintegrate. Reduce heat, add soy, and stir for 5–10 minutes. Add sesame oil and stir for another 2 minutes. Season with pepper.

Trim each lettuce leaf to form a piece with sides measuring 4–5″ (10–12.5cm). Be guided by the shape of the leaves. Near the stalk end, the pieces will form a cup shape. Place a spoonful of fish mixture onto each lettuce piece and arrange on a serving dish. Serve at room temperature.

TOASTED JAPANESE SCALLOPS

Makes 24

12 large scallops,
    without roe, thawed if
    frozen
6 tbsp light soy
3 tbsp mirin
1 tbsp sake
1 tsp Japanese pepper
    (kona sansho)
red pepper squares for
    serving, optional
flat-leaved parsley for
    garnish, optional

Wash scallops and pat dry with kitchen
paper. Cut them in half. Mix soy, mirin
and sake in a pan. Simmer for 2 minutes,
remove from heat, add scallops and leave to
marinate for 10 minutes.

Drain scallops and pat dry. Thread 4 at a
time onto long metal skewers. Grill 5″
(12.5cm) under a fairly high heat for 4
minutes, turning to cook evenly and basting
with soy mixture. Slide scallops off the
skewer, sprinkle very lightly with japanese
pepper and garnish with flat-leaved parsley if
liked. Serve warm on a platter or squares of
red pepper. Eat with cocktail sticks.

CLASSIC CHINESE PRAWNS

Makes 30

1 1/2 lb (700g) medium
 raw prawns, thawed if
 frozen, peeled and
 deveined
3/4 tsp sea salt
groundnut or corn oil
 for deep-frying
4 cloves garlic, finely
 chopped
2 tsp finely chopped
 fresh ginger
2 fresh green chillies,
 seeded and chopped
4 large spring onions,
 white parts only, cut
 into small rounds
5 stems coriander,
 leaves coarsely
 chopped, stems cut
 into 1" (2.5cm)
 pieces
sweet chilli sauce for
 dipping

Put prawns in a large bowl, sprinkle with
salt and mix well. Leave to stand for 20
minutes.

Add oil to a wok and heat to 180°C/350°F.
Slide in prawns and deep-fry for 30 seconds.
Remove with a slotted spoon and pat dry
with kitchen paper.

Drain oil from the wok leaving 2 tbsp.
Add garlic, ginger and chilli, stir and then
add spring onion and stir. Return prawns to
the wok and sauté for about 1 minute until
cooked, turning once. Mix in coriander and
remove from heat. Serve warm with sweet
chilli sauce for dipping.

GOLDEN PRAWN BALLS

Makes 20

1 lb (450g) medium raw
prawns, thawed if
frozen, peeled and
deveined, with tails
intact
6 canned water
chestnuts, finely
chopped
2oz (50g) pork fat,
finely minced

½ tsp caster sugar
1 tsp salt
1 tsp cornflour
1 egg white, lightly
beaten
6–8 slices stale white
bread, crusts
removed, cut into very
tiny croutons
corn oil for deep-frying

Put prawns in a food processor and finely
chop. Transfer to a bowl with water
chestnuts, pork fat, sugar and salt, sprinkle
over cornflour and mix well. Add egg white
and stir vigorously for 2 minutes until
mixture has an elastic texture. Refrigerate
for ½ hour.

Spread bread cubes on a tray. Roll about
1 tbsp of prawn paste into a ball, then roll on
bread cubes until more or less covered.
Repeat until paste is finished.

Add oil to a wok and heat to 180°C/350°F.
Add balls and deep-fry for 2–3 minutes until
golden. Remove and drain on kitchen paper.
Serve hot.

SWEET AND SOUR FISH

Makes 24

1½lb (700g) cod fillet
seasoned flour
corn oil for deep-frying

BATTER
9oz (250g) plain flour
pinch salt
2 tbsp corn oil
½pt (300ml) water
1 egg
3 egg whites

SAUCE
1½ tbsp tomato
  ketchup

5 tsp red wine vinegar
2 tsp light soy
3 tsp soft brown sugar
3 tbsp water
2 tbsp corn oil
6oz (175g) raw peeled
  shrimps, thawed if
  frozen
4oz (100g) button
  mushrooms, stalks
  removed
1 dried chilli, deseeded
  and finely chopped
3 slices fresh ginger
1½ tsp cornflour, mixed
  with 4 tsp water
seasoning

Make batter: mix flour and salt in a bowl, and gradually add oil and water. Mix in egg and chill for ½ hour.

Meanwhile, make sauce: mix ketchup, vinegar, soy, sugar and water in a bowl. Heat oil in a pan and stir-fry shrimps for 30 seconds. Add other sauce ingredients.

Dry fish with kitchen paper. Cut into 24 pieces, 3 × 2″ (7.5 × 5cm) and dust with seasoned flour. Whisk egg whites until stiff and fold into batter.

Heat oil in a wok to 180°C/350°F. Dip fish in batter and deep-fry for 5 minutes until light and golden. Serve warm with sauce.

DEEP-FRIED SOFT-SHELL CRABS

Makes 20

*20 soft-shell crabs,
thawed if frozen
1oz (25g) cornflour
1oz (25g) plain flour
4floz (100ml) water
corn oil for deep-frying
lime for garnish,
optional*

Pat dry crabs with kitchen paper and set aside. Combine cornflour and flour in a bowl and slowly add the water, stirring as you do so to a smooth batter.

Heat a wok containing oil over high heat to 180°C/350°F. Dip crabs lightly into batter, coating completely. Drop into hot oil and deep-fry in batches for 2–3 minutes until light golden. Drain on kitchen paper and serve immediately, garnished with lime slices and zest if liked.

CRUNCHY JELLYFISH SKINS

Makes 25

8oz (225g) dried
  jellyfish skin pieces,
  soaked in cold water
  for 4 hours
1 cucumber, cut in half
  lengthwise
3 tbsp very finely
  chopped spring
  onions for garnish
1 red pepper, deseeded
  and cut into fine strips
  for garnish

DRESSING
½ tsp soft brown sugar
½ tsp salt
1 tbsp black sweetened
  vinegar
1 tbsp light soy
2 tsp sesame oil

Rinse soaked jellyfish well before use. Bring a pan of salted water to the boil, plunge in jellyfish, leave for 30 seconds and drain. Leave to cool and then cut into about 25 thin 3–4" (7.5–10cm) strips.

Combine dressing ingredients in a bowl and toss with jellyfish strips. Leave for 20 minutes.

Deseed cucumber and cut into quarters lengthwise. Slice each quarter to form little 'boats' about 1½" (3.5cm) long and serve lined with a few strands of jellyfish. Garnish with spring onion and strips of red pepper. Serve cold.

ASPARAGUS AND CRABMEAT TARTLETS

Makes 30

30 filo tartlets
  (p. 153)
4 tbsp corn oil
2 tsp finely chopped
  fresh ginger
1 lb (450g) asparagus,
  ends trimmed, cut
  diagonally into ¼"
  (5mm) slices
1 tbsp shaosing wine or
  dry sherry
½ tsp salt

¼pt (150ml) chicken
  stock
1 tsp finely chopped
  garlic
4 spring onions, white
  parts only, cut into
  very fine rounds
8oz (225g) crabmeat,
  thawed if frozen
1 tsp cornflour
¼pt (150ml) water
3 tbsp oyster sauce

Make filo tartlets (p. 153). Heat a wok over high heat, add about 2 tbsp of oil, add ginger and then asparagus. Stir-fry for 2 minutes. Splash in wine and then add salt and stock. Bring to the boil and simmer for 4 minutes until asparagus is slightly tender. Remove asparagus with a slotted spoon, drain and keep warm.

Add about 2 tbsp oil to the wok and stir-fry garlic and spring onion. Throw in crabmeat and stir. Blend cornflour, water and oyster sauce together, add to the wok and mix well. Leave to thicken and then return asparagus to the wok.

Spoon a little asparagus mixture into each wonton tartlet and serve warm.

FISH TEMPURA

Makes 12–15

corn oil for deep-frying
1 1/2lb (700g) white fish
  fillets, sliced into 1 1/2"
  (4cm) squares
12 raw prawns, peeled,
  deveined, with tails
  intact
12oz (350g)
  courgettes, sliced
12 mushroom caps

BATTER
1 egg
1/2pt (300ml) water
7oz (200g) plain flour
2 1/2oz (65g) cornflour
salt

SAUCE
1/2pt (300ml) chicken
  stock
2 tbsp light soy
2 tbsp mirin

F irst make batter: whisk egg and water in
a bowl. Gradually add flour, cornflour
and salt. Lightly beat and chill for 1 hour.
  Meanwhile, mix sauce ingredients
together in a pan and simmer for 2 minutes.
  Heat oil in a wok to 170°C/325°F. Dip fish
pieces, prawns and vegetables into batter
and deep-fry until golden, 1–2 minutes.
Drain and serve immediately with sauce.

STEAMED FISH PARCELS

Makes 24

1 ½lb (700g) thick
  white fish fillets
2 tsp turmeric
2 tsp salt
3 small onions, chopped
2 cloves garlic, chopped
1 tsp powdered ginger
½ tsp chilli powder
1 tbsp ground rice
4floz (100ml) coconut
  milk
1 tbsp corn oil
12 leaves chinese
  cabbage
raffia lengths for tying

C ut fish into 24×1″ (2.5cm) cubes.
Rub with half of turmeric and salt
and put to one side. Purée onions and garlic in
a food processor. Add ginger, chilli, rice and
any remaining salt and turmeric and process
for 30 seconds. Mix in coconut milk and oil,
and blend for 15 seconds.

Cut each leaf in half across its width.
Spread some paste in centre of each half.
Place a fish piece on top and spread with
more paste. Fold up into parcels and tie
with raffia. Place in a steamer and steam
over a pan of boiling water for
15–20 minutes. Serve warm.

MARINATED MACKEREL

Makes 30

2lb (900g) fresh
   mackerel fillets
2 tsp salt
7floz (200ml) white
   wine vinegar
4 tbsp caster sugar
4 carrots, peeled
4oz (100g) white
   radish, peeled
4 tbsp wasabi paste

SOY DIP
7floz (200ml) white
   wine vinegar
2 tbsp caster sugar
8floz (225ml) light soy
6 tbsp finely chopped
   fresh ginger

Cut fish fillets diagonally into strips 1½"
(4cm) wide and place in a bowl.
Sprinkle with salt and refrigerate for 4
hours. Remove fish and wipe off salt with a
cloth. Mix vinegar and sugar with fish and
refrigerate again for ½ hour. Slice carrots
and radish into fine julienne.

Mix dip ingredients together in a pan.
Simmer for 3 minutes then leave to cool.

To serve, arrange fish with chopped
vegetables and wasabi and soy dip alongside.

GRILLED CLAMS

Makes 8–16

8 large or 16 small
  clams, in shells
sea salt

S oak clams overnight in cold salted
water, rinse and drain. Roll clams in salt
and grill 4–5" (10–12.5cm) under a moderate
heat for 2 minutes or until they open. Serve
on plates coated with salt (sea salt if
possible).

SASHIMI

Serves 20

*12oz (350g) fresh
mackerel, filleted*

*12oz (350g) fresh
halibut, filleted*

*12oz (350g) fresh tuna
steaks*

*8oz (225g) carrots,
peeled*

8oz (225g) celery

8oz (225g) cucumber

*2oz (50g) horseradish
powder (wasabi),
mixed with 4 tbsp
cold water*

4 tbsp light soy

1 tbsp english mustard

2 tbsp dark soy

*1 tbsp finely chopped
fresh ginger*

C ut mackerel and halibut into very thin
diagonal slices ½ × 1″ (1 × 2-5cm).
Cut tuna into straight ¼″ (5mm) diagonal
slices. Cut carrot, celery and cucumber into
fine julienne.

Lay out fish and vegetables in an
attractive pattern on a serving plate. Spoon
on wasabi at the side. Combine light soy and
mustard together, and then dark soy and
ginger, and serve as 2 dipping sauces. Guests
can dab each fish piece with a little wasabi,
roll them up with a little vegetable and dip
them into the sauces. Serve at room
temperature.

Glazed Salmon

Serves 10

12oz (350g) salmon, in
   3 steaks
1/2 tsp salt
1 tbsp cornflour
1/2 tbsp lightly beaten
   egg white
2 tbsp vegetable oil
2 tbsp light soy
1 1/2 tsp caster sugar
5 tsp mirin
coriander for garnish

Cut salmon into small bite-size cubes and place in a bowl. Add salt, cornflour and egg white and combine well. Leave to marinate for 40 minutes. Drain salmon from marinade.

Place a wok over medium heat and add oil. Add salmon and brown on both sides, about 1 minute each side, gently scooping fish around the wok. Add soy, sugar and mirin and leave to reduce slightly so that the sauce thickens and coats the fish.

Remove from the wok with a slotted spoon and place on a platter. Garnish with coriander. Eat with cocktail sticks.

HOT AND SOUR SQUID

Serves 15

8oz (225g) dried squid
    pieces, body only,
    soaked for 1 hour
1pt (575ml) cold water
2 tsp orange juice
2 tsp salt
2 tsp cornflour
corn oil for deep-frying
4oz (100g) lean pork
    steak, shredded
2 tbsp finely chopped
    canned bamboo
    shoots
¼ leek, shredded
1 tsp chilli powder
2 tbsp light soy
2 tbsp rice wine vinegar

Drain soaked squid and remove the membrane and bone. Cut each piece in half lengthwise. Make criss-cross slashes on the insides then cut into ¾" (1cm) slices. Place in a bowl and pour over boiling water. When the slices curl up, drain and cover again with the cold water and orange juice. Soak for ½ hour.

Rinse squid completely. Rub each piece with salt, then dust with cornflour. Heat oil in a wok to 180°C/350°F and deep-fry squid for 30 seconds. Drain on kitchen paper.

Drain wok to leave 2 tbsp oil. Replace over medium heat. Add pork, bamboo shoots, leek and chilli, and stir-fry for 2–3 minutes. Add squid again and then soy and vinegar; stir-fry for a further 1–2 minutes.

When sauce has thickened transfer to a warm serving dish. Eat with cocktail sticks.

PHOENIX PRAWNS

Makes 20

1 lb (450g) medium raw
  prawns, thawed if
  frozen, peeled,
  deveined, with tails
  intact
½ tsp salt
corn oil for deep-frying

BATTER
5oz (150g) plain flour
5 tbsp cornflour
1 ½ tsp baking powder
7fl oz (200ml) water
½ tsp salt
1 tbsp corn oil

Make batter: put flour and cornflour and
baking powder into a large bowl.
Gradually whisk in water and blend until
smooth. Add salt and oil and leave for
½ hour.

Cut undersides of prawns to straighten
them out. Sprinkle with salt. Add oil to a wok
and heat to 180°C/350°F. Hold each prawn by
its tail and coat the body in batter. Deep-fry
in batches for about 3 minutes until pale
golden. Drain on kitchen paper and serve
warm.

PRAWNS WRAPPED IN RICE PAPER

Makes 30

1lb (450g) medium raw
   prawns, thawed if
   frozen, peeled,
   deveined, with tails
   intact
1 egg white, lightly
   beaten
1 tsp salt
½ tsp caster sugar
2 tsp cornflour

2oz (50g) pork fat,
   finely chopped
3oz (75g) lean ham,
   finely chopped
4oz (100g) canned
   bamboo shoots, finely
   chopped
4–6 spring onions, cut
   into tiny rounds
15 sheets rice paper
corn oil for deep-frying
chilli sauce for dipping

Chop prawns roughly and put in a bowl. Add egg white, salt, sugar and cornflour and mix until prawns are well coated. Add pork fat, ham and bamboo shoots and stir well. Mix in spring onion.

Cut each rice paper sheet into 2 × 4″ (10cm) squares. Place on a flat surface. Spread 1 tbsp filling onto each square, almost to the edges. Fold over and roll up, leaving both ends open; moisten ends with water and seal.

Heat oil in a wok to 190°C/375°F. Deep-fry in batches for about 3 minutes until cooked and rice paper is crisp. Remove and drain on kitchen paper. Serve hot with chilli sauce for dipping.

SCALLOP-STUFFED MANGE-TOUT

Makes 25

8oz (225g) mange-tout
1 lb (450g) scallops,
  thawed if frozen
1 tbsp minced fresh
  ginger
1 tbsp minced spring
  onion
1 tbsp shaosing wine or
  dry sherry
1 tsp salt
1 tsp sesame oil
½ egg white, lightly
  beaten
1 tbsp cornflour
4oz (100g) raw
  shrimps, thawed if
  frozen, finely diced
3 lemons, cut into
  wedges for serving

Lightly rinse mange-tout and scallops and pat dry with kitchen paper. Using a sharp knife, split open one side of each mange-tout. Dice 4oz (100g) of scallops.

Put remaining scallops in a food processor and purée. Add ginger, spring onion, wine, salt, sesame oil and egg white and process to blend all together.

Transfer mixture to a bowl and add cornflour, mixing vigorously in one direction until stiff and pasty. Fold in diced shrimp and scallops and chill for 1 hour.

Spoon scallop mixture into mange-tout, and arrange them in a steamer that has first been lined with greaseproof paper and lightly brushed with sesame oil. Steam mange-tout over a wok of boiling water for 5–7 minutes until scallop mixture is firm to touch. Serve warm with wedges of lemon.

STIR-FRIED SCALLOPS

Serves 12

*1 1/2lb (700g) scallops,
preferably fresh*
2 tbsp corn oil
*8 cloves garlic, finely
chopped*
*3 spring onions, white
parts only, cut into
tiny rounds*
1/2 tsp salt
black pepper
*2 tsp shaosing wine or
dry sherry*
1 tbsp light soy
1/2 tsp soft brown sugar

U sing a sharp knife, carefully remove scallops from shells. Separate the roe. Cut any large scallops in half. Rinse both scallops and roe under cold water, drain and pat dry with kitchen paper. This needs to be done thoroughly.

Heat a wok over high heat and add oil then garlic and spring onion. Stir for 1 minute. Add scallops with roe and stir. Add salt and pepper. Stir for 1 more minute, then splash in wine. Wait until it has stopped sizzling then add soy and sugar. Stir for 1 more minute.

Remove from the wok with a slotted spoon and serve warm with cocktail sticks.

PRAWN SUSHI

Makes 6

6 large raw prawns,
  peeled, deveined,
  with tails intact
6 toothpicks
2floz (50ml) rice wine
  vinegar

1½ tsp soft brown
  sugar
½ tsp salt
3 large eggs
1 egg yolk

S lit underside of each prawn along length
and splay out. Straighten curve of
prawns by inserting toothpicks across middle
through inside curve. Drop them into a pan
of boiling water and cook for 2 minutes until
pink. Drain well and remove toothpicks. Cut
through prawns lengthwise, then open and
flatten them lightly with the flat blade of a
large knife.

In a bowl mix rice vinegar with 1 tsp of
sugar and ¼ tsp of salt. Add prawns and
leave to marinate for 1 hour. Drain and set
aside.

Meanwhile, in a small pan, combine eggs,
egg yolk, ½ tsp sugar and ¼ tsp salt. Stir
well and cook over low heat until egg is
lightly set. Remove from heat and press
mixture through a sieve. Divide egg mixture
into 6 equal pieces and squeeze each gently
to form small patties.

Place a prawn on each egg patty, cut-side
down. Arrange on a plate and serve cold.

DEEP-FRIED SQUID

Makes 50

1 1/2lb (700g) baby
  squid, thawed if
  frozen
1/4 tsp 5-spice powder
1pt (575ml) corn oil for
  deep-frying
1/2 fresh green chilli,
  very finely shredded
a little sesame oil
a little soft brown sugar

MARINADE
2 tbsp dark soy
2 tbsp hoisin sauce
1 tbsp shaosing wine or
  dry sherry
2 tbsp golden syrup
2 tsp fresh ginger juice
1 tsp cornflour
1/4 tsp salt
white pepper to taste

S eparate heads from bodies of squid
under running water. Discard glutinous
membranes. Cut down the length of the
bodies, score the surfaces in a criss-cross
pattern and cut each crosswise into 4 pieces.

  Mix marinade ingredients together in a
bowl. Add squid pieces and mix thoroughly.
Leave for at least 2 hours. Then, drain in a
sieve and sprinkle with 5-spice.

  Heat oil in a wok to 170°C/325°F. Add
squid and fry for 1 minute. Remove with a
slotted spoon. Now heat a wok or frying pan
with just 2 tbsp of oil to a very high heat. Add
squid again and chilli and stir-fry for 2
minutes. Add a drop of sesame oil and sugar
to taste. Stir-fry again quickly and serve hot.

Chicken & Duck

A wonderful range of classic
and original chicken, quail and
duck ideas.

There are a variety of inspirations for the recipes in this chapter, in particular China and Japan. They differ in flavour intensity, so choose according to your requirements – the Chinese chicken dishes tend to be more highly spiced whereas the Japanese dishes (such as chicken sashimi) are more subtle. Duck is an important oriental bird, and features highly here.

Most of the recipes use chicken breasts, which can be bought pre-packaged. If you buy them with the wings attached, separate the wings from the breasts with a sharp knife by cutting through the connecting joint; wings are a favourite oriental delicacy and can also be found in this chapter.

Several of the recipes can be prepared in advance: some, such as bang-bang chicken tartlets, Hunan chicken drumsticks, Cantonese chicken wings and black bean chicken, actually benefit from being made beforehand. Many of the recipes include a short marinating time, which is well worth adhering to as the flavour and texture of the food is greatly improved. However, no items here take a lot of effort, and some – such as chicken in paper – require only last-minute preparation and cooking.

Eat these items with your fingers or with cocktail sticks or bamboo skewers. Have a pretty selection of small bowls for serving the dipping sauces, and a ready supply of napkins if you think it is necessary.

CHICKEN IN PAPER

Makes 30

2 skinned chicken
   breast fillets
4 spring onions, white
   and green parts
   separated, cut into
   ½" (1cm) pieces
2 tsp finely chopped
   fresh ginger

1 tbsp dry sherry
2 tbsp light soy
1 tsp salt
1 tsp soft brown sugar
30 × 3" (7.5cm)
   square pieces edible
   rice paper
a little beaten egg
vegetable oil for deep-
   frying

Slice chicken widthways into 30 oblongs,
½ × 1" (2 × 2.5cm), and put in a bowl.
Add spring onion, ginger, sherry, soy, salt and
sugar and marinate for 30–40 minutes.

Grease rice paper squares and place a
piece of chicken into the centre of each.
Wrap by folding three corners into centre of
paper to form an 'envelope'. Fold up flap so
that it doubles up, and tuck it in. Seal with
egg. Half-fill a pan with oil and heat to
180°C/350°F. Deep-fry in batches for about 2
minutes until golden. Drain and serve hot.

Chicken Yakitori

Makes 40

2 skinned chicken
  breast fillets
5oz (150g) chicken
  livers
2 tbsp oil
1/2 green and 1/2 yellow
  pepper, cut into
  squares
1 onion, roughly diced

MARINADE
1/4pt (150ml) sake or
  dry sherry
1/4pt (150ml) light soy
1 tbsp caster sugar
1 tbsp finely chopped
  fresh ginger

C ut chicken into 40 pieces roughly 1/2″ (1cm) square. Cut livers into similar sized pieces, suitable for threading onto skewers.

Rub a little oil onto skewers and thread a chicken piece, liver and cubes of pepper and onion onto each one.

Mix marinade ingredients in a small pan and bring to the boil and remove from heat. Lay skewers in a low flat dish and pour over marinade. Leave for 15–30 minutes, turning at intervals.

Grill in dish under a medium heat for 3–4 minutes, basting frequently, turning once, until cooked through. Serve hot.

CHICORY WITH CHICKEN AND PLUM SAUCE

Makes 30

2 skinned chicken
  breast fillets
4oz (100g) canned
  bamboo shoots
1 tsp soft brown sugar
2 tbsp dark soy
2 tbsp plum sauce
½ tsp salt
1 tsp cornflour
2 tbsp shaosing wine or
  dry sherry
3 tbsp corn oil
1 tsp chopped garlic
3 tomatoes, peeled,
  deseeded and
  chopped
2 tbsp water
30 chicory leaves

Slice chicken and bamboo shoots into short, fine julienne. Put chicken in a bowl with sugar, 1 tbsp of soy, plum sauce, salt, cornflour and 1 tbsp of shaosing wine; marinate for ½ hour.

Heat a wok over high heat until smoke rises, add 1 tbsp of oil and add garlic, bamboo and tomato. Stir for about 30 seconds, and remove from wok with a slotted spoon.

Reheat the wok, add remaining oil and then add chicken. Stir well to separate. Cook for 2–3 minutes, add remaining soy and wine, add water, then bamboo mixture. Stir for 1 more minute and then take off heat and cool.

Fill chicory leaves near the root with the cooled mixture. Refrigerate for ½–1 hour before serving.

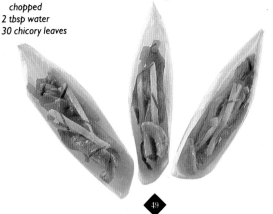

PEKING DUCK

Makes 30

4–6lb (1.8–2.75kg)
  oven-ready duckling
5 tbsp hoisin sauce
30 mandarin pancakes
  (p.152)
10 spring onions, white
  parts only, cut into 1"
  (2.5cm) pieces then
  shredded
1/4 cucumber, cut into
  1/4" (5mm) slices then
  finely shredded

MARINADE
1 tbsp black treacle
2 tbsp runny honey
1/2pt (300ml) boiling
  water
1/2pt (300ml) shaosing
  wine or dry sherry
1/2 tsp salt
2 tsp finely chopped
  fresh ginger
2 tbsp soft brown sugar

Wash and clean duck, and dry inside and out with kitchen paper. Mix marinade ingredients together in a bowl. Immerse duck and leave to marinate for 5–8 hours. Hang duck with string by its neck from a hook (over a tray to catch drips) for at least 10 hours until completely dry.

Place duck, breast downwards, in a preheated 200°C/400°F/Gas 6 oven; on the lower rack place a roasting tin three-quarters full of water. Roast for 45 minutes, then turn over and roast for another 45 minutes. Baste frequently with hoisin sauce. Turn up the heat to highest setting for 10 more minutes to make skin brown and and crispy.

Carve duck into very thin slices. To serve, spread each pancake with a little hoisin, add a little spring onion and cucumber, place on slices of duck and fold over. Serve hot or cold.

DRUNKEN CHICKEN

Makes 20

2 skinned chicken
  breast fillets
1 tsp finely chopped
  fresh ginger
2 spring onions, white
  and green parts
  separated, cut into
  ½" (1cm) pieces
2 tsp salt
5 tbsp shaosing wine or
  dry sherry
poppy seeds for garnish,
  optional
cucumber sticks for
  garnish, optional

Drop chicken into a pan with ½pt
(300ml) of boiling water. Add ginger,
spring onion and salt. Cover and simmer for
10 minutes. Turn off heat and leave chicken
soaking in liquid for ½ hour or until cool.

Slice chicken thinly. Put into a bowl and
pour over wine. Place in the refrigerator and
leave for 24 hours.

Drain chicken. Press edges in poppy
seeds if liked and garnish with cucumber.
Serve chicken on a platter with some of its
liquid, and eat with cocktail sticks.

Quails with 5-Spice

Makes 12

2 tbsp runny honey
1/2pt (300ml) hot, not
  boiling, water
2 tsp rice wine vinegar

6 small oven-ready
  quails
chinese seasoned salt
vegetable oil for frying
fine strips green spring
  onion for garnish

Melt honey in water in a pan over
medium heat and add vinegar. Baste
quails with this liquid. Tie legs of quails
together with string and hang them from a
hook over a tray for 2–3 hours so that the
basted liquid dries onto them.

Cut birds down and rub them inside and
out with seasoned salt, using 1/2 tsp per bird.
Heat oil in a wok to 190°C/375°F and
deep-fry birds in batches for 4–5 minutes
until crispy. Drain on kitchen paper.

Split birds in half down centre with a
heavy knife. Serve warm, garnished
with spring onion and with seasoned
salt for dipping.

STUFFED CHICKEN WINGS

Makes 24

2oz (50g) canned
  bamboo shoots
24 chicken wings
2–3 oz (50–75g) ham,
  thickly sliced
vegetable oil for deep-
  frying
sweet chilli sauce for
  dipping, optional

MARINADE
1½ tsp salt
2 tbsp light soy
1 tsp honey
1 tsp shaosing wine or
  dry sherry
1 tsp cornflour dissolved
  in 1 tsp water
black pepper

S lice bamboo shoots fairly thickly. Blanch
  in boiling water for 30 seconds then
refresh under cold water. Drain and cut into
strips about 1″ (2.5cm) long.

Bone chicken wings: hold upright and cut
around central bones, pulling skin down off
meat as you do so. Remove bones and pull
skin up again. Cut ham into 24 strips, 1 ×
¼″ (2.5 × 0.5cm). Take a piece of ham and
bamboo shoot and insert them into a boned
wing. Fold any skin at the open ends inwards
to form a parcel. Stuff the rest of wings.

Mix marinade ingredients in a bowl, add
wings and leave for an hour, turning once.

Half-fill a wok with oil and heat to
180°C/350°F. Remove chicken wings from
marinade and deep-fry for 3–5 minutes until
brown and crispy and thoroughly cooked.
Remove with a slotted spoon and serve hot
with chilli sauce for dipping if liked.

HUNAN CHICKEN DRUMSTICKS

Makes 15

15 chicken drumsticks
2 tbsp sesame paste
1 tbsp rice wine vinegar
1 tbsp sesame oil
1 tsp chilli oil
1 tbsp dark soy
1 tsp szechuan pepper,
  finely crushed
2 tsp finely chopped
  fresh ginger
4–6 spring onions, very
  finely chopped
1 tbsp chopped garlic
1 tsp chilli powder
sesame seeds, optional

Bring a wok containing water to the boil and add drumsticks. Cook for 10–15 minutes until cooked through. Drain and leave to cool.

Combine all remaining ingredients in a large bowl and add the chicken drumsticks. Refrigerate for 2–3 hours and then drain. Dip ends of drumsticks in sesame seeds if liked and serve cold.

SPICED CHICKEN LIVERS

Makes 64

1 lb (450g) chicken
  livers
1 tbsp vegetable oil
2 tsp finely chopped
  fresh ginger
2 spring onions, white
  and green parts
  separated, cut into
  1/2" (1cm) pieces
1 dried chilli, deseeded
  and finely chopped
2 tbsp dry sherry
3 tbsp light soy
1 tbsp soft brown sugar
1 tsp 5-spice powder
4 tbsp water

Remove fat from livers and quarter each one. Heat a wok until smoke rises, add oil and then chicken livers. Stir-fry for 2 minutes over a medium heat, taking care not to break livers. Stir in ginger, spring onion and chilli, then splash in sherry. Wait for the sizzling to die down and add soy, sugar and 5-spice. Add cold water and simmer for 10–15 minutes.

Remove from wok and leave to cool. Slice and serve with cocktail sticks.

Note: The livers are especially good if prepared the day before and left in the sauce.

BANG-BANG CHICKEN TARTLETS

Makes 30

2 skinned chicken
  breast fillets
½pt (300ml) chicken
  stock
30 filo tartlets (p.153)
6 spring onions, white
  parts only, finely
  shredded
¼ cucumber, cut into
  ¼" (5mm) slices then
  finely shredded for
  garnish

DRESSING
1 tbsp sesame paste
2 tbsp light soy
1 tsp rice wine vinegar
2 tsp soft brown sugar
2 tsp chilli oil
black pepper
2 tsp sesame oil

Put chicken in a pan and pour over stock.
Bring to the boil and simmer for 15–20
minutes until cooked through. Drain and
leave to cool. Make filo tartlets (p.153).
  Combine dressing ingredients in a bowl.
Peel off shreds of chicken with your fingers.
Mix together the chicken and spring onion
and put small amounts into each tartlet.
Pour over a little dressing and serve cold,
garnished with a little cucumber.

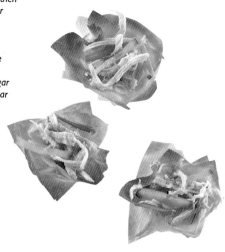

CHICKEN SASHIMI

Makes 24

2 skinned chicken
  breast fillets
½ tsp salt
¾ cucumber, thinly
  sliced
2 large tomatoes,
  peeled, deseeded and
  cut into strips
1 tsp soft brown sugar
3 tbsp sweet yellow
  bean paste
2floz (50ml) chicken
  stock
1 egg yolk
½ tsp japanese or
  english mustard
1 tsp rice wine vinegar

Lightly flatten chicken between sheets of greaseproof paper with a rolling pin and sprinkle with salt. Leave to stand for 5 minutes.

Bring a pan of water to the boil and poach breasts for 4 minutes. Transfer them immediately to a bowl containing iced water and cool for 3 minutes. Drain and pat dry with kitchen paper. Chill in the refrigerator for ½ hour, and chill cucumber and tomato at the same time.

Combine sugar, bean paste, stock and egg yolk in a small pan. Put on a low heat and stir very well without boiling. Add mustard and vinegar, remove from heat and stir well.

Cut each breast into 24 very thin ½" (1cm) long slices. Spread a tiny amount of paste onto each cucumber slice and top with chicken, cucumber and tomato.

GLAZED CHICKEN BALLS

Makes 24

8oz (225g) skinned
  chicken fillet
2 tbsp plain flour
1 tsp light soy

1 egg
1 tsp soft brown sugar
2 tbsp mirin
2 tsp poppy seeds
2 tsp sesame seeds
24 cocktail sticks

Put chicken into a food processor and process until a smooth paste. Add flour, soy and egg and process again for a few seconds. Form paste into about 24 small bite-size balls.

Bring a wok containing ¾pt (450ml) water to the boil and drop in the balls, a small batch at a time. Poach them for 3–4 minutes, then add sugar and mirin. Simmer uncovered until liquid is reduced and chicken balls are coated with glaze.

Roll balls in poppy and sesame seeds and press onto cocktail sticks.

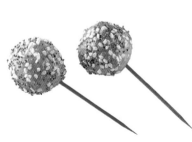

SZECHUAN DUCK PANCAKES

Makes 30

4–5lb (1.8–2.25kg)
    oven-ready duckling,
    thawed if frozen
2 tbsp szechuan pepper
3 tbsp salt
2 tbsp finely chopped
    fresh ginger
2 tbsp dark soy
2 tbsp 5-spice powder
groundnut oil for deep-
    frying
30 mandarin pancakes
    (p.152)
nori strips for garnish,
    optional

Wash duck well and dry thoroughly with kitchen paper inside and out. Grind pepper and salt together in a mortar until fine. Mix with ginger, soy and 5-spice. Rub duck all over, in and out, with this mixture, then cover and refrigerate for 6 hours.

Place duck in a preheated 150°C/300°F/ Gas 2 oven and on the lower shelf place a roasting tin three-quarters full with cold water. Roast for 1½–2 hours, topping up water if necessary. Remove duck from oven and wipe inside and out with kitchen paper to remove any moisture.

Heat oil in a wok to 180°C/350°F and deep-fry duck until brown and crispy. Drain and slice the flesh very finely.

Put a few slices duck in centre of each pancake. Fold up into parcels, wrap up with nori if liked, and serve hot.

CHICKEN SATAY

Makes 30

3 skinned chicken
  breast fillets
2 red peppers, cut into
  ¾" (1cm) squares
6 spring onions, cut into
  ¾" (1cm) lengths
30 cocktail sticks

MARINADE
3 shallots, finely
  chopped
1 tsp finely chopped
  garlic
2 tbsp light soy
1 tsp ground coriander
1 tsp ground ginger
1 tbsp lemon juice
1 tbsp corn oil

SAUCE
4oz (100g)
roasted peanuts
2 shallots, finely
  chopped
1 tsp finely chopped
  garlic
1 tbsp corn oil
8floz (225ml) water
1 tbsp lemon juice
1 tsp soft brown sugar

Cut chicken into 60 small ½" (1cm) square pieces. Combine ingredients for marinade in a bowl. Add chicken and leave for 3 hours.

Thread 2 pieces chicken, pepper and spring onion pieces onto each skewer (about 5–6 items per stick in total).

Prepare sauce by processing peanuts in a food processor until fine. Sauté shallots and garlic in oil in a pan, add water and bring to the boil. Add ground peanuts, lemon juice and sugar. Boil for about 5–6 minutes until sauce thickens and remove from heat.

Grill skewers under a medium heat for 3–4 minutes, turning once or twice, and serve with sauce.

HOISIN CHICKEN

Makes 40

2 skinned chicken
  breast fillets
vegetable oil for deep-
  frying
3 cloves garlic, finely
  chopped
4 spring onions, white
  and green parts
  separated, cut into
  ½" (1cm) pieces
1 tbsp shaosing wine or
  dry sherry
3 tbsp hoisin sauce

MARINADE
1 tbsp shaosing wine or
  dry sherry
2 tsp cornflour
1 tbsp lightly beaten
  egg white
1 tsp salt

Cut chicken into about 40 rough ¾"
(2cm) cubes. Put in a bowl and add
marinade ingredients. Mix together with a
fork and leave for ½ hour.

Heat a wok until smoke rises and add oil.
Add garlic and white part of spring onion,
then stir in chicken cubes with marinade.
Cook for about 3–4 minutes, scooping the
ingredients around the wok with a spatula,
then splash in wine. Cook for another 2–3
minutes then remove chicken with a
slotted spoon.

Add hoisin to the wok and some water if
you think the consistency is too thick. Add
chicken once again, and throw in green
spring onion. Stir to glaze chicken with
sauce and serve in a bowl.

DUCK-STUFFED LYCHEES

Makes 40

3 skinned duck breast
  fillets, thawed if
  frozen
3 pieces dried tangerine
  peel, softened for ¹/₂
  hour in warm water
  then drained
1 tbsp finely chopped
  fresh ginger
1 tbsp finely chopped
  duck fat
2 tbsp light soy
2 tbsp shaosing wine or
  dry sherry
1 tbsp sesame oil
1 tbsp potato flour
black pepper
3 × 1lb2oz (500g)
  cans lychees, drained
  well
coriander for garnish

Put duck breasts into a food processor.
Cut up peel into small squares and add
to bowl. Process to a smooth paste. Add
ginger and process, then add duck fat and
process again. Add all remaining ingredients
apart from lychees and process for 20
seconds. The mixture should be a thick
paste.

Put paste into a piping bag and pipe a
little into each lychee. Line a steamer with
moistened muslin or greaseproof paper and
pack in the lychees.

Fill a wok or pan large enough to fit the
steamer with water, and bring to the boil.
Cover and steam lychees for about 20
minutes. Serve warm, garnished with
coriander.

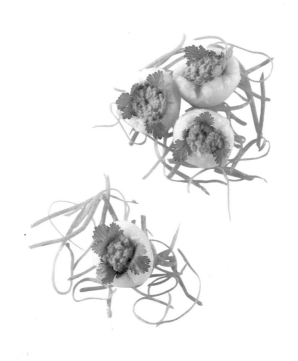

DEEP-FRIED CHICKEN WONTONS

Makes 35

3 skinned chicken
  breast fillets
1 ½ tbsp light soy
1 tbsp shaosing wine or
  dry sherry
½ tsp salt
2 tsp sesame oil
1 tsp 5-spice powder
2 tsp finely chopped
  fresh ginger
2½oz (65g) canned
  water chestnuts,
  finely chopped
6 spring onions, white
  parts only, very finely
  sliced
1 tbsp potato flour
35 wonton wrappers
plain flour for dusting
vegetable oil for deep-
  frying
worcester sauce or
  sweet chilli sauce for
  dipping

Put chicken into a food processor and process to a coarse paste. Blend in soy, wine, salt, oil, 5-spice and ginger. Transfer to a bowl, add water chestnuts and spring onions and stir thoroughly. Sprinkle over potato flour and mix well.

Take a wonton wrapper. Place 1 tsp chicken mixture in the centre. Fold wrapper over gently in half to form a triangle. With the top pointing upwards, gently twist the base of the wrapper around the filling to form a small bag. Moisten neck of twisted wrapper to ensure it stays together. Repeat for remaining wontons. Dust them lightly with flour to prevent sticking.

Heat a wok until smoke rises. Add oil and heat to 180°C/350°F. Deep-fry until golden. Drain and serve hot with dipping sauce.

ALMOND-COATED CHICKEN SKEWERS

Makes 30

3 skinned chicken
    breast fillets
30 cocktail sticks
3oz (75g) plain flour,
    plus extra for dusting
2 eggs, lightly beaten
4oz (100g) flaked
    almonds, finely
    chopped
vegetable oil for deep-
    frying

MARINADE
2 tbsp light soy
2 tbsp shaosing wine or
    dry sherry
1 tsp sesame oil
1 tsp 5-spice powder
1 tbsp finely chopped
    fresh ginger
2 tbsp finely
    chopped spring
    onions
1 tsp finely
    chopped garlic
black pepper

Cut chicken into 60 cubes roughly ¾"
(2cm). Place in a bowl and add
marinade ingredients. Stir and leave for
3–4 hours.

Thread 2 pieces chicken onto each of 30
cocktail sticks, leaving a slight gap between
pieces. Place flour, eggs and almonds in
separate dishes and dip skewers into each in
turn – flour, eggs then almonds. Place on a
flour-dusted tray and leave to dry for 1 hour.

Heat a wok until smoke rises, add oil and
heat to 180°C/350°F. Add skewers, 3 or 4 at a
time, and deep-fry for 4–5 minutes until
golden and cooked through. Remove and
drain on kitchen paper. Serve warm.

BLACK BEAN CHICKEN

Makes 30

3 skinned chicken
  breast fillets
1 tbsp corn oil
2 cloves garlic, finely
  chopped
4 spring onions, cut into
  tiny rounds, white
  parts only
2 tbsp fermented black
  beans, rinsed and
  mashed

1 tbsp yellow bean
  sauce
1 tsp light soy
1 tsp shaosing wine or
  dry sherry
1/2 tsp salt
black pepper
1 tsp potato flour,
  dissolved in 2 tbsp
  cold water

Flatten each chicken breast between
greaseproof paper with a rolling pin and
set aside.

Heat a wok over high heat, add oil and
swirl around. Stir in garlic, then spring
onions. Scoop around the wok and add black
beans, yellow bean sauce and soy. Stir for
1–2 minutes. Splash in wine and wait for
sizzling to stop. Add salt and pepper. Stir in
potato flour dissolved in water and cook for 1
more minute. Spread sauce over flattened
chicken breasts and leave to cool.

Roll up breasts tightly, wrap in tinfoil and
refrigerate for 1 hour. Then, poach in a pan
of boiling water for 6–8 minutes. Drain and
leave to cool. To serve, unwrap and slice into
1/4" (5mm) thick rounds.

CANTONESE CHICKEN WINGS

Makes 20

20 chicken wings, tips
    removed
1 egg, lightly beaten
4 tbsp potato flour
8 spring onions, very
    finely chopped
vegetable oil for deep-
    frying

MARINADE
2 tbsp dark soy
1 tbsp shaosing wine or
    dry sherry
1 tsp soft brown sugar
1 tsp sesame oil
3 cloves garlic, finely
    chopped
1 tbsp finely chopped
    fresh ginger

C ombine marinade ingredients with
chicken and leave for 1 hour or more.

Drain and coat wings well in a bowl with
beaten egg. Lightly dredge them with potato
flour and leave on a tray to dry for about 1
hour. Roll in spring onion to cover.

Heat a wok until smoke rises and add oil
for deep-frying. Heat to 180°C/350°F and add
half of wings. Cook for about 5 minutes until
crispy and cooked through. Repeat with
remaining wings. Drain and serve hot.

Beef, Pork & Lamb

Dark and savoury to light and spicy, here are meat recipes with a difference.

Y ou will find both simple and elaborate
meat ideas in this chapter, ranging from
flavoured strips of marinated beef to tiny
dumplings that contain tasty mixtures of
pork and spices. Some items are quite well
known in the West, such as beef and spring
onion rolls; others such as char sui pork
slices may look plain but have a wonderful
flavour when eaten. Traditionally, meat is
regarded as such a delicacy in China and the
Orient that it is usually served with little
garnish, either just in slices or sometimes
covered in a thin glaze. There are a number
of bright garnishes to liven up the serving
plate if you desire.

You will not need to buy special cuts of
meat for the recipes in this chapter, and
should be able to find most of the ingredients
in any large supermarket. It is important to
follow the marinating times in the recipes as
this process gives the meat a better texture
and additional succulence.

Marinating can of course be done in
advance, as can most of the general
preparation. However, you are advised to
leave any roasting and grilling until just
before serving for best results. Some recipes
such as minty lamb balls or meatballs with
grated lime peel can be made the day before,
covered with cling film and refrigerated until
required. Pork and shrimp wontons and
other dumplings can be made in large
batches and frozen.

GINGER-GLAZED PORK

Makes 25–30

2lb (900g) pork
    tenderloin, cut into
    chunks
4 tsp ginger juice
4 tsp sake
8 tbsp light soy
2 tbsp vegetable oil
4 tbsp mirin
4 tsp soft brown sugar
2 tbsp water
baby sweetcorn for
    serving, optional

Put pork in a bowl. Mix ginger juice, sake and 4 tbsp of soy, pour over pork and marinate for 1 hour.

Heat vegetable oil in a heavy frying pan and sauté pork for 4 minutes; reduce heat and cook for a further 5 minutes. Transfer meat to a plate.

Add mirin, remaining soy, sugar and water to the pan. Simmer for 2 minutes. Return pork to the pan and cook over a high heat for 2 minutes.

Serve warm or cold in a bowl. Eat with cocktail sticks. Baby sweetcorn is a good accompaniment, if liked.

GRATED LIME MEATBALLS

Makes 50–60

1 lb (450g) rump beef
¾ tsp salt
½ tsp soft brown sugar
1½ tbsp dark soy
black pepper
1 tsp ginger juice
2 tsp shaosing wine or
  dry sherry
2 tsp potato flour or
  arrowroot
4 tbsp water
10 canned water
  chestnuts, finely
  chopped
2 large pieces dried
  lime peel, finely
  grated
1 tbsp sesame oil
3½–4 fl oz (90–
  100ml) groundnut or
  vegetable oil
4 large cloves garlic,
  crushed
sweet chilli sauce for
  dipping
lime rind for garnish,
  optional

Mince beef in a food processor until almost puréed. Transfer to a bowl. Add salt, sugar, soy, pepper, ginger, wine and flour and mix thoroughly. Add water, 1 tbsp at a time, stirring until smooth after each addition. Add water chestnuts, lime peel, sesame oil and 1½ tbsp of groundnut oil and mix thoroughly.

Scoop up 1½ tsp of mixture at a time and roll into a ball; repeat to make 50–60 balls.

Heat half remaining oil in a sauté pan; when it is very hot, add garlic and fry until brown. Remove from pan and discard. Reduce the heat, add meatballs in batches and cook for 3 minutes, turning to ensure they are cooked all over. Serve hot, garnished with lime if liked, and with sweet chilli sauce for dipping.

GARLIC SPARE RIBS IN BLACK BEAN SAUCE

Makes 60

3lb (1.35kg) spare ribs

MARINADE
6 tbsp fermented black
  beans, rinsed and
  mashed
3 fresh chillies,
  deseeded and diced

2 tbsp very finely
  chopped garlic
¾ tsp salt
1 ½ tsp soft brown
  sugar
6 tbsp light soy
6 tbsp shaosing wine or
  dry sherry
6 tsp sesame oil

C hop spare ribs into about 60×1″
(2.5cm) lengths with a chopper or
heavy knife. Mix all marinade ingredients
together in a bowl, add spare ribs and leave
for 1 hour.

Transfer ribs to a wire rack and put in a
preheated 190°C/375°F/Gas 5 oven with a
roasting tin half-full of water placed on a
lower shelf. Cook for 10 minutes. Heat
marinade and pour over ribs to serve.

BEEF AND GINGER SKEWERS

Makes 40

10oz (275g) lean rump
  beef
3" (7.5cm) piece fresh
  ginger, peeled and
  very thinly sliced
8 spring onions, cut into
  1" (2.5cm) pieces
20 bamboo skewers

MARINADE
3floz (75ml) water
2 tbsp light soy
2 tbsp mirin
2 tbsp shaosing wine or
  dry sherry
1 tsp soft brown sugar

C ut beef into 40 very thin ½×1" (1"
2.5cm) slices. Combine marinade
ingredients in a bowl, add beef and leave for
½ hour. Stir at intervals.

    Thread beef, ginger and spring onion
alternately onto each skewer. Grill under a
medium heat for 2–3 minutes, basting
regularly with marinade. Serve warm or
chilled.

SHAO-MAI DUMPLINGS

Makes 30

1 lb (450g) pork steak
6oz (175g) raw peeled
  shrimps
2oz (50g) canned
  water chestnuts,
  finely chopped
6 dried chinese black
  mushrooms,
  reconstituted, stems
  removed and caps
  finely chopped
30 dumpling wrappers
light soy for dipping
fresh chilli strips for
  garnish, optional

SEASONING
2 tsp light soy
1 tbsp shaosing wine or
  dry sherry
1 tsp salt
2 tsp sesame oil
1/2 tsp soft brown sugar
1/4 tsp black pepper
1 tbsp minced spring
  onions
2 tsp minced fresh
  ginger
1 egg white, lightly
  beaten
1 1/2 tbsp cornflour

Put pork in a food processor and process until smooth. Lightly chop ground pork until fluffy. Put in a bowl. Mince shrimps to a coarse paste in a food processor and add to pork with the water chestnuts, black mushrooms and all seasonings. Mix thoroughly.

Put a heaped tbsp of filling in the middle of one dumpling wrapper and gather up the edges (keeping remaining wrappers covered with a damp cloth). Holding the dumpling between your fingers, lightly squeeze it in the centre to form a waist. Push up filling from the bottom of the dumpling to create a flat surface. Smooth top surface with the underside of a spoon dipped in hot water. Make remaining dumplings in the same way, and arrange in a steamer lined with lightly oiled greaseproof.

Fill a wok with water so it is level with the bottom edge of the steamer, and heat until boiling. Steam dumplings in batches for 15 minutes over high heat.

Remove and serve warm with soy sauce for dipping. Press in chilli strips if liked.

BEEF TARTLETS WITH OYSTER SAUCE

Makes 30

12oz (350g) lean rump
   beef, cut into very
   thin ½" (1cm) square
   pieces
30 filo tartlets (p.153)
1 tsp vegetable oil
1 tsp finely chopped
   garlic
1 tsp finely chopped
   fresh ginger
3 spring onions, white
   and green parts
   separated, cut into
   tiny rounds
1 tbsp shaosing wine or
   dry sherry
4 tbsp water
2 tbsp oyster sauce
1 tsp cornflour
white spring onion strips
   for garnish

MARINADE
½ tsp salt
½ tsp soft brown sugar
2 tsp dark soy
1 tbsp shaosing wine or
   dry sherry
1 tsp cornflour
1 tbsp water

C ombine marinade ingredients in a bowl,
   add beef and leave for ½ hour. Make
tartlets (p. 153).

   Heat a wok until smoke rises. Add
vegetable oil and then garlic, ginger and
spring onion. Add beef and stir-fry for 2
minutes. Splash in wine and stir.

   Mix together water, oyster sauce and
cornflour and add to the wok, stirring well.
Scoop beef and sauce into each tartlet,
garnish with spring onion and serve warm.

LIME-FLAVOURED SPARE RIBS

Makes 40

3lb (1.35kg) spare ribs
salt and white pepper
2 eggs, beaten
plain flour for dusting
1 ½pt (875ml) corn oil
    for deep-frying
lime slices for garnish

MARINADE
3 ½floz (90ml)
    chinese red or malt
    vinegar
4 tbsp soft brown sugar
½ tsp salt
¼ tsp black pepper
1 ½ tsp dark soy
finely grated zest and
    juice 3 limes

C hop spare ribs into about 40×3″
(7.5cm) lengths and season.

In a bowl, mix together marinade
ingredients, add spare ribs and leave to
marinate for several hours.

Dip spare ribs into beaten egg, then dust
with flour.

Heat oil in a wok or deep-fryer to
140°C/275°F and deep-fry ribs in batches for
2 minutes until cooked and golden in colour.
Drain and serve hot, garnished with lime
slices.

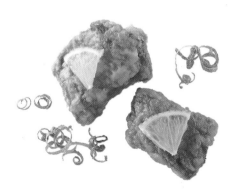

PORK AND SHRIMP WONTONS

Makes 70

10oz (275g) pork
  steak, chopped
2oz (50g) pork fat,
  finely chopped
6oz (175g) shrimps,
  finely chopped
1 tsp salt
½ tsp soft brown sugar
2 tbsp light soy
1 tbsp shaosing wine or
  dry sherry
1 tsp cornflour
2 tbsp water
6 dried chinese
  mushrooms,
  reconstituted
5oz (150g) bamboo
  shoots, finely chopped
8 spring onions, sliced
  into thin rounds
1 egg yolk
1 tbsp sesame oil
70 wonton wrappers
corn oil for deep-frying

SAUCE
3 tbsp corn oil
1 tbsp sesame oil
6 tbsp light soy
2 tbsp water

Put pork in a food processor and mince finely. Transfer to a bowl and mix in pork fat, shrimps, salt, sugar, soy, wine and cornflour. Slowly add water and stir well. Throw pork mixture with your hands around the bowl quite vigorously for 3–4 minutes. Slice mushrooms finely. Mix with bamboo shoots and spring onion, then blend in sesame oil. Add egg yolk to bind mixture.

Round off edges of wonton wrappers with scissors. Put a tsp of pork mixture into the centre of each wrapper. Fold over to form a semi-circle, pinch the wrapper to secure and cover until ready to use.

Put sauce ingredients in a pan and mix well. Bring to the boil and simmer over a low heat for 3 minutes.

Bring a wok containing water to the boil. Cook wontons in 2 batches for 3–4 minutes until cooked through. Drain and serve with warm sauce.

CURRY BEEF TURNOVERS

Makes 24

1 tbsp vegetable oil
2 cloves garlic, finely
  chopped
8oz (225g) rump beef,
  very finely diced
1 onion, finely chopped
1 tbsp light soy
2 tsp curry powder
½ tsp soft brown sugar
8 sheets filo pastry
1 egg yolk, lightly
  beaten

Heat a wok over high heat until smoke rises, add oil, then garlic, beef and onion. Stir-fry for 2 minutes. Add soy, curry and sugar. Remove from heat and cool.

Divide filo pastry into 2 sets of 4 sheets placed on top of each other. Cut each 'stack' into 4 long strips of equal proportions. Put a small amount of beef at the beginning of a strip and fold one corner of the pastry over diagonally to form a small triangle. Cut the triangle off and seal the edges with some egg yolk. Continue until all pastry is used up, to make about 3 per strip. Brush with egg yolk.

Bake in a preheated 190°C/375°F/Gas 5 oven for 10 minutes until golden. Serve warm.

CHAR SIU SLICES

Makes 36

2lb (900g) boned blade
    or leg of pork, without
    skin
4 tbsp runny honey

MARINADE

3 tbsp hoisin sauce
2 tbsp yellow bean
    sauce
4 tbsp light soy
4 tbsp soft brown sugar
2 tbsp shaosing wine or
    dry sherry

Cut pork into 3 or 4 pieces of even size.
Make 3 deep cuts into each piece from
opposite sides without cutting completely.

Combine marinade ingredients in a bowl,
add pork and leave for about 4 hours, turning
frequently.

Preheat an oven to 190°C/375°F/Gas 5.
Drain pork and place on the top rack of the
oven; below place a roasting tray three-
quarters full with water. After 30–40 minutes
remove each pork piece and dip in remaining
marinade. Replace in the oven, lower the
temperature to 150°C/300°F/Gas 2 and roast
for a further ½ hour.

Remove pork and brush generously with
honey. Leave to cool. Cut each piece of pork
into 9–12 thin slices and serve warm or cold.

DRIED PEPPER BEEF

Makes 30–40

1 lb (450g) lean beef, skirt or sirloin
2 tbsp corn oil
1 tbsp finely chopped fresh ginger
2 spring onions, white parts only, cut into 1/2" (1cm) pieces

4 tbsp shaosing wine or dry sherry
3 tbsp soft brown sugar
2 tbsp light soy
1 tsp 5-spice powder
black pepper
2 red peppers, deseeded and cut into small triangles for garnish

Cut beef into 30–40 strips, 1/4" (5mm) wide and 2" (5m) long. Heat a wok until smoke rises, add oil and then ginger and spring onion. Be careful not to burn. Add beef and stir for 2 minutes.

Add all remaining ingredients and stir well. Reduce the heat, cover and simmer for 20–25 minutes. If there is still some liquid remaining at the end of this time then turn up the heat to evaporate.

Pick out spring onion and discard. Spread contents of the wok in a low dish and leave to cool. Dry out further in a very low oven, about 100°C/200°F/Gas 1/4, for 20 minutes; then cover and leave in the refrigerator overnight. Serve cold, garnished with red pepper triangles, on cocktail sticks.

Red Crispy Pork

Makes 40

40 mange-tout, topped
1 tbsp corn oil
2lb (900g) boned pork
  shoulder
1 tbsp finely chopped
  spring onion
1 tbsp finely chopped
  fresh ginger
2 tsp shaosing wine or
  dry sherry
1 tsp salt
1 tsp szechwan pepper,
  crushed
2 tbsp rice wine vinegar

B lanch mange-tout in boiling water with
corn oil for 30 seconds. Drain, refresh
under cold running water and pat dry with
kitchen paper. Put to one side.

Cut pork into small ¼×2½″ (0.5×
6cm) thin oblongs. Bring a pan of water to
the boil, drop in pork and simmer for 2–3
minutes. Drain.

Put into a steamer, sprinkle on all
remaining ingredients except vinegar, and
place over a wok of boiling water. Steam,
covered, for about 15 minutes until cooked.
Discard spices, wipe pork dry with kitchen
paper and leave to cool.

Roast pork on a tray in a preheated
200–220°C/400–425°F/Gas 6–7 oven for 10–15
minutes. Remove and brush with vinegar
several times. Stuff into mange-tout
when cold.

PORK AND VEGETABLE BUNS

Makes 30

DOUGH
3 tbsp caster sugar
5 tbsp warm water
1 tsp active yeast
powder
6 tbsp plain flour
1 oz (25g) lard, cut into
small pieces

FILLING
1 lb (450g) pork steak,
minced
½ chinese cabbage,
finely chopped
½ tsp salt
1 tsp finely minced
fresh ginger
¼ tsp caster sugar
3 tbsp light soy
1 tbsp sesame oil
1 tsp potato flour
8 spring onions, white
parts only, cut into
thin rounds
fresh chilli strips,
optional

First make dough: mix sugar and warm water in a small bowl. Sprinkle over yeast and stir. Place flour in another small bowl, add lard and work to fine breadcrumbs with your fingers. Make a well in the centre and pour in yeast mixture. Stir with a wooden spoon. Turn onto a flat surface and knead to a smooth elastic dough. Cover the bowl with a cloth and leave in a warm place for 3 hours to double in size. Turn onto a floured surface.

Mince pork in a food processor, transfer to a bowl and add all filling ingredients. Mix well and leave to stand while dough is being rolled out.

Roll dough into a long roll about 1" (2.5cm) in diameter. Cut roll in half and then cut each half into about 15 equal slices. Form each piece into a ball, then roll each ball into 3" (7.5cm) circles.

Put 2 tsp filling into centre of each circle and gather up sides. Insert strips of chilli into tops if liked. Twist slightly at the tops to seal. Arrange buns in a steamer, placed slightly apart, and leave for ½ hour to rise.

Put the steamer over a wok containing boiling water and steam over a high heat for 20–25 minutes. You will probably need to steam buns in 2–3 batches. Remove and serve slightly warm.

SPICY LAMB AND SWEET BEAN PANCAKES

Makes 30

1½lb (700g) boned leg
of lamb
6 tbsp corn oil
6 spring onions, finely
shredded
30 mandarin pancakes
(p.152)

MARINADE
1 tbsp sweet bean
sauce
1 tbsp light soy
2 tsp rice wine vinegar
½ tsp sweet chilli sauce
2 tsp soft brown sugar
3–4 tbsp water

SAUCE
1 tbsp light soy
3 tsp rice wine vinegar
1 tsp sesame oil
2 cloves garlic, finely
chopped
½ tsp finely chopped
fresh ginger
1 tbsp water
1 tsp potato flour

Cut lamb into ¾" (2 cm) cubes and then into matchstick threads. Combine marinade ingredients in a bowl, add lamb and leave for ½ hour. Combine sauce ingredients together in a bowl.

Heat a wok until smoke rises. Add oil and heat to 180°C/350°F. Add lamb and stir-fry for 5–7 minutes until the pieces separate and change colour. Add spring onions and stir for 1 minute. Remove lamb and onion and set aside.

Heat sauce ingredients in a small pan. Remove from heat, add lamb shreds and toss. Spread each pancake with a little sauce and a few shreds of lamb. Fold over and serve warm.

MINTY LAMB BALLS

Makes 24

12oz (350g) lamb
 steak
2oz (50g) pork fat,
 finely minced
1 egg white
1 tbsp light soy
½ tsp salt
1 tsp soft brown sugar
1 tsp cornflour
4 spring onions, cut into
 thin rounds
2 tbsp finely chopped
 mint
plain flour for dusting
vegetable oil for deep-
 frying
chopped mint for
 rolling, optional

GLAZE
2 tsp light soy
2 tsp shaosing wine or
 dry sherry
1 tsp sweet chilli sauce
1 tsp hoisin sauce
2 tsp corn oil

Cut lamb into large pieces and mince in a
food processor. Add pork fat and
process until combined. Add egg white, soy,
salt, sugar, cornflour, spring onion and mint.
Process briefly again. Transfer to a bowl and
roll mixture into about 24 bite-sized balls.
Dust lightly with flour.

Heat a wok until smoke rises. Add oil and
heat to 180°C/350°F. Add balls, a few at a
time, and deep-fry for 2–3 minutes until light
brown and cooked through. Drain.

Combine glaze ingredients in a pan. Bring
to the boil, stirring frequently. Remove from
heat, add balls and toss to coat. Roll some in
mint if liked and serve warm.

PORK SPRING ROLLS

Makes 80

10oz (275g) lean pork
  tenderloin
3 dried chinese
  mushrooms,
  reconstituted
1 lb (450g) bean sprouts
2 spring onions, cut into
  tiny rounds
1 tbsp dark soy
1 tsp cornflour
1 tsp soft brown sugar
¾ tsp salt
corn oil for deep-frying
2 cloves garlic, finely
  chopped
2 tsp finely chopped
  fresh ginger
1 pkt spring roll
  wrappers, quartered
½ tbsp beaten egg

Cut pork into matchsticks and chop mushrooms finely. Put pork, mushroom, bean sprouts and spring onion in a bowl with soy, cornflour, sugar and salt. Mix thoroughly and leave to marinate for ½ hour.

Heat 2 tbsp of oil in a wok over high heat, add garlic and ginger and stir for a few seconds. Add pork with marinade and stir-fry for 3–4 minutes until pork is cooked and most of liquid evaporated. Remove

mixture from the wok and leave to cool.

Place 1 tsp filling off-centre on a wrapper quarter. Fold up bottom corner over filling. Tuck in side edges and roll up completely, sealing with some beaten egg. Cover and make remaining spring rolls in the same way.

Heat oil in a wok to 180°C/350°F, drop in spring rolls a few at a time and deep-fry for 2–3 minutes until golden. Drain on kitchen paper and serve warm.

LION'S HEAD

Makes 20

MEATBALLS
1¼lb (650g) lean pork
    tenderloin
2oz (50g) pork fat
6 canned water
    chestnuts
3 spring onions, white
    parts only, finely
    chopped
1½ tbsp shaosing wine
    or dry sherry
1 egg, lightly beaten
2 tsp cornflour
1½ tsp finely chopped
    fresh ginger
1½–2 tsp soft brown
    sugar
¼ tsp black pepper
½ tsp salt
chinese leaves for
    serving

SAUCE
1 tsp cornflour
½pt (300ml) chicken
    stock
1 tsp soft brown sugar
3 tsp light soy
4 tsp shaosing wine or
    dry sherry

Mince pork fat and finely chop water
chestnuts. Mix with all other meatball
ingredients in a bowl. Leave to marinate for 1
hour. Form mixture into about 20 tiny
equal-sized balls.

Heat 2 tbsp oil to a high temperature in a
frying pan and fry balls on both sides for 5
minutes until lightly browned. Set aside.
Blend cornflour with a little water, add to
stock and mix with remaining sauce
ingredients in a bowl. Add to pan and simmer
for 25 minutes over low heat. Set aside.

Coat balls in sauce and serve in chinese
leaves.

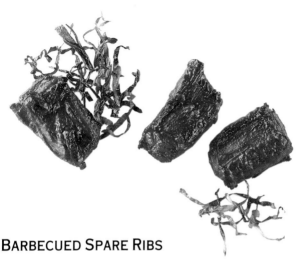

BARBECUED SPARE RIBS

Makes 35

3lb (1.35kg) spare ribs

MARINADE
3 tbsp hoisin sauce
3 tbsp light soy
3 tbsp shaosing wine or
  dry sherry
3 tbsp soft brown sugar
2 tbsp tomato ketchup
6 cloves garlic, finely
  chopped

C hop ribs into 35 rough 3″ (7.5cm) lengths with a chopper or heavy knife. Bring a large pan of water to the boil and drop in ribs. Simmer over a medium heat for 15 minutes.

Combine marinade ingredients in a bowl and stir in spare ribs. Refrigerate for at least 4 hours.

Put ribs onto a baking tray and cover with marinade. Bake in a preheated 180°C/350°F/Gas 4 oven for 30–35 minutes. Serve warm.

PEARLY PORK BALLS

Makes 30

10oz (275g) boned
pork shoulder

6oz (175g) white
  glutinous rice
1 tbsp dried shrimps,
  soaked in boiling
  water for 15 minutes
  and drained
6 canned water
  chestnuts, finely
  chopped

6 dried chinese
  mushrooms,
  reconstituted and
  diced very finely
1 tbsp cornflour
seasoning
3–4 tbsp water
3oz (75g) lean ham,
  diced very finely

C hop pork coarsely and mince in a food
processor. Soak rice in cold water for 2
hours and drain well.

Finely chop shrimps and combine in a
bowl with water chestnuts, mushrooms and
minced pork. Add cornflour and seasoning.
Blend in water, but be sure not to make the
mixture too runny.

Mix ham with rice and spread out on a
tray. Roll about 2 tsp of pork mixture at a
time into a ball and then roll over the rice
and ham so that rice sticks to the balls.

Place slightly apart in a steamer (you will
need to cook in batches) and steam over a
wok of boiling water for about 15 minutes.

BEEF AND SPRING ONION ROLLS

Makes 30

2lb (900g) topside beef
6 tbsp dark soy
3 tbsp mirin
3 tsp grated fresh
  ginger

12 spring onions,
  white parts only, cut
  into 1½" (4cm)
  pieces
plain flour for dusting
vegetable oil for deep-
  frying

C ut beef into about 30 paper-thin slices
and place in a bowl. Combine soy, mirin
and ginger and pour over beef. Marinate for
½ hour.

Lift beef out of marinade and lay on a flat
surface. Lay spring onion pieces widthways
over beef slices, leaving a small margin at
each end, and roll up. Dab flour on end of
each beef strip to hold the rolls together.
Coat entire rolls with flour.

Half-fill a wok with oil and heat to
180°C/350°F. Cook rolls, a few
at a time, for 3 minutes. Drain on
kitchen paper and serve hot.

BACON AND OYSTER PUFFS

Makes 32

4 cakes bean curd,
    about 2 × 2½"
    (5 × 6cm) square,
    drained
vegetable oil for deep-
    frying
6 rashers streaky bacon
4oz (100g) canned
    smoked oysters,
    coarsely chopped
pepper
finely chopped
    coriander for garnish

Quarter each cake of bean curd and pat dry with kitchen paper. Heat oil in a wok to 190°C/375°F. Deep-fry bean curd pieces in batches for 10–13 minutes. Each piece will float when ready. Drain on kitchen paper.

Grill bacon until well done. Chop finely and mix with smoked oyster in a bowl. Grate some black pepper into mixture.

Cut each bean curd piece in half horizontally and fill each with bacon and oyster mixture. Serve warm or cold garnished with coriander.

BACON-WRAPPED WATER CHESTNUTS

Makes 20–24

10–12 rashers streaky
  bacon
1 tbsp runny honey,
  dissolved in 1½ tbsp
  hot water
2×6oz (175g) canned
  water chestnuts (20–
  24), drained
20–24 cocktail sticks

Using a pastry brush, brush one side only
of each bacon rasher with honey
solution. Cut each rasher in half widthways,
and wrap a bacon piece, honey-side in,
around each chestnut. Secure with cocktail
sticks.

Place on a baking sheet, join sides down,
place under a hot grill and cook for 2–3
minutes. Turn and cook for 2 minutes more.
The bacon should be well cooked and slightly
crispy. Serve warm.

Vegetables

*Full of texture and flavour, a feast of
vegetable party delights.*

U nlike Western party menus, vegetables form a crucial part of the Far Eastern table, chosen in their own right for texture and flavour rather than as a vehicle for carrying other ingredients. Marinated and braised vegetables feature highly: pickled Peking cabbage and marinated vegetables are two examples given here. They also act well as palate cleansers between fish and meat items.

Most of the vegetables in this chapter can be found in any greengrocer or supermarket, with the exception of some more unusual items such as taro or sweet potato which can be found in oriental shops.

You can prepare many of these items in advance. Vegetables can be marinated; dried mushrooms can be soaked and braised; vegetarian spring rolls can be rolled and deep-frozen before being deep-fried: just remove them from the freezer about four hours beforehand, keep them covered while defrosting and then deep-fry at the last minute. Vegetable tempura, on the other hand, achieve best results when the batter is prepared just before deep-frying.

It is unnecessary to be too elaborate with garnishes as this section is so naturally colourful. However, there is lots of scope for decoration if you wish – for example: tie up bundles of marinated vegetables with thin strips of spring onion greens to make little bundles. For real authenticity, use bamboo or citrus leaves to lay the food on.

STEAMED LEMON AND GINGER ASPARAGUS

Serves 15

3lb (1.35kg) fresh
  asparagus

DRESSING
1 tbsp finely grated
  fresh ginger

3 tbsp lemon juice
4floz (100ml) corn oil
1 tbsp sesame oil
1 tsp salt
¼ tsp white pepper

Make dressing: mix ginger and lemon juice in a bowl. Whisk vigorously, adding oil in a slow stream. As mixture starts to thicken, add oil at a faster rate. Fold in sesame oil, salt and pepper and set aside.

Wash and trim woody ends of asparagus. Place in a steamer and cook over a pan of boiling water for 10 minutes or until just tender. They should be just 'al dente'. Place in a dish, toss with dressing and serve at room temperature.

TARO AND SWEET POTATO CHIPS WITH TWO SAUCES

Serves 10

8oz (225g) sweet
  potato
1lb (450g) taro
vegetable oil for deep-
  frying

AVOCADO DIP
2 ripe avocados, peeled
  and stoned
1½ tbsp lemon juice
¼ tsp chilli sauce
¼pt (150ml) carton
  yogurt
½ tsp salt

SWEET CHILLI DIP
1 tbsp corn oil
1 clove garlic, finely
  chopped
2 spring onions, white
  parts only, cut into
  tiny rounds
2 tsp sweet chilli sauce
1 tsp shaosing wine or
  dry sherry
2 tsp light soy
3 tbsp crème fraiche
juice ½ lemon

Make avocado dip: purée avocados in a food processor. Add lemon juice, chilli sauce, yogurt and salt and process until thick and creamy. Transfer to a dish and chill.

Make sweet chilli dip: heat a wok over high heat until smoke rises, and add oil. Add garlic and spring onion, and stir-fry for 20 seconds. Add chilli sauce, splash in wine and soy, and stir well. Remove from heat. Empty crème fraiche and lemon juice into a small bowl and combine well. Chill for ½–¾ hour.

Peel sweet potato, slice into very thin rounds, rinse under cold running water and pat dry on kitchen paper. Peel taro and slice into fine julienne. Do not rinse.

Half-fill a wok with oil and heat to 190°C/375°F. Drop potato rounds into oil, keeping them separate, and fry for 3 minutes until light golden. Remove with a slotted spoon and drain on kitchen paper. Fry taro chips in same way. Serve chips hot or cold with the sauces.

PICKLED AUBERGINE

Serves 10–15

2 aubergines, 8–10oz
   (225–275g) each
2¼pt (1.3ltr) water
1½ tbsp salt

DRESSING
1½ tbsp dry mustard
6 tbsp light soy
6 tbsp mirin
6 tbsp soft brown sugar

Cut ends off aubergines and cut each in
half lengthwise. Slice each half into ⅛"
(3mm) semi-circular slices, then cut each
slice in half again. Put in a bowl with water
and salt and leave for 1 hour. Drain
aubergines and lay on kitchen paper. Pat dry
thoroughly.

Combine all dressing ingredients in a
bowl and whisk thoroughly. Add aubergines,
cling film and refrigerate for about 4 hours.

When ready to serve, remove aubergines
from dressing with a slotted spoon and dab
dry with kitchen paper. Arrange on a platter
and pour over a little dressing.

STUFFED OKRA

Makes 36

8oz (225g) skinned
   chicken breast fillets
1 tbsp dark soy
$\frac{1}{2}$ tsp cornflour
1 tbsp plum sauce
$\frac{1}{2}$ tsp soft brown sugar
2 dried chinese black
   mushrooms,
   reconstituted

12oz (350g) canned
   bamboo shoots
36 okra
1$\frac{1}{2}$ tbsp corn oil
1 tbsp shaosing wine or
   dry sherry
salt and white pepper

Dice chicken into $\frac{1}{8}$" (3mm) pieces and
place in a bowl with soy, cornflour, plum
sauce and sugar. Mix thoroughly and leave to
marinate for $\frac{1}{2}$ hour. Meanwhile dice
mushrooms and bamboo shoots to same size
as chicken.

Lay each okra flat, and using a very sharp
knife, slit each lengthwise and remove seeds.
Blanch them in boiling salted water for 10
seconds, refresh under cold running water,
drain and then dry inside and out with
kitchen paper.

Heat oil in a wok to a high heat. Add
chicken to oil and stir-fry for 1 minute. Now
add wine, bamboo shoots and mushrooms
again and continue to stir-fry for another
minute. Adjust seasoning and set aside.

When mixture has cooled, fill okra
carefully and arrange on a serving platter.
Serve cold.

VEGETARIAN SPRING ROLLS

Makes 100

10oz (275g) dried
  cellophane noodles
1lb (450g) carrots,
  finely shredded
5 sticks celery, cut into
  matchsticks
15 dried chinese
  mushrooms,
  reconstituted
4 tbsp groundnut or
  vegetable oil
4 cloves garlic, finely
  chopped
2 tsp finely chopped
  fresh ginger
8oz (225g) frozen
  sliced french beans,
  thawed and dried
1 tsp salt
3 tbsp light soy
1 pkt 8″ (20cm) square
  spring roll wrappers
1 egg white, lightly
  beaten
vegetable oil for deep-
  frying
worcester or chilli
  sauce for dipping

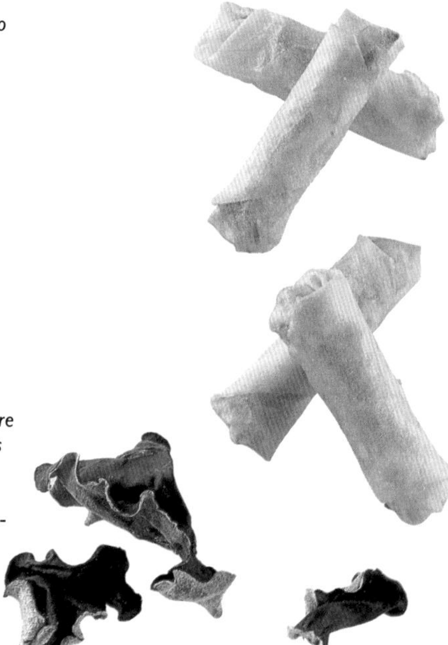

Put cellophane noodles in a large bowl and pour over 2pt (1.15ltr) boiling water. Cover and leave for ½ hour. Drain well and cut up roughly. Blanch carrots and celery separately in boiling water, drain and rinse in cold water. Drain and pat dry with kitchen paper. Drain mushrooms and shred into fine slivers.

Heat oil in a wok. Add garlic and ginger; when garlic takes on colour, add carrots, mushrooms and celery, then cellophane noodles, and stir-fry for 1 minute. Add french beans and continue to stir-fry over reduced heat until excess water has evaporated. Season with salt and soy.

Peel off a batch of spring roll wrappers and quarter them. Separate and spread about 2 tsp of vegetable mixture onto each quarter, just off-centre. Fold the bottom corner over filling, tucking in the sides. Roll up, folding the side flaps into the centre as you go. Seal with egg white. Quarter remaining wrappers and repeat for rest of rolls.

Half-fill a wok or deep-fryer with oil and heat to 180°C/350°F. Deep-fry rolls for 3–4 minutes until pale golden. Remove with a slotted spoon and drain on kitchen paper. Serve hot with worcester or chilli sauce for dipping.

VEGETABLE TEMPURA

Serves 15

1/4 cauliflower
4oz (100g) broccoli
1 red pepper, deseeded
4oz (100g) baby
  sweetcorn, tops
  removed
1 aubergine, cubed
4oz (100g) okra, tops
  removed
vegetable oil for deep-
  frying
1 tbsp light soy
1 tbsp worcester sauce

BATTER
1 large egg
4oz (100g) plain flour
4floz (100ml) water

Separate cauliflower and broccoli into bite-sized florets, and cut pepper into strips. Blanch sweetcorn for 3 minutes in boiling water, drain and set aside.

Make batter: break egg into a bowl and beat lightly until foamy. Add flour, then slowly add water, mixing until smooth.

Fill a wok or deep-fryer a third full with vegetable oil and heat to 180°C/350°F. Dip vegetables into batter then deep-fry until light golden brown, separating them as they cook with chopsticks. Remove with a slotted spoon and drain on kitchen paper. Continue until all vegetables are cooked, skimming oil after each batch.

Arrange tempura on 2 platters. Sprinkle soy over one and worcester sauce over other.

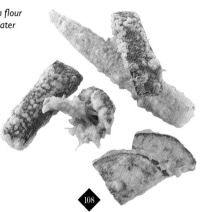

MARINATED VEGETABLES

Serves 10

8oz (225g) carrots
4 sticks celery (4oz/
    100g)
I white radish (8oz/
    225g)
8oz (225g) broccoli
I red pepper (6oz/
    175g), deseeded
4oz (100g) emmental,
    very thinly sliced

MARINADE
about ¼pt (150ml)
    water
½pt (300ml) dry white
    wine
3 tbsp olive oil
1½ tbsp white wine
    vinegar
juice and grated zest
    I lime
½ tbsp fresh ginger
    juice
2 cloves garlic, finely
    chopped
2 tsp soft brown sugar
2 sprigs mint
½ tbsp salt
4 coriander seeds
½ tbsp turmeric

Cut carrots, celery and white radish into julienne, separate broccoli into florets and slice red pepper into strips.

Place all marinade ingredients in a large pan, bring to the boil and simmer for 5 minutes. Add carrot, celery and radish and simmer, covered, for 5 minutes. Add broccoli and pepper and simmer for a further 3 minutes. Transfer to a large bowl and leave to cool for 2 hours. Refrigerate overnight.

An hour before serving, drain vegetables and dry off with kitchen paper. Lay on a platter with emmental; to eat, wrap a cheese slice around a pickled vegetable.

SESAME SPRING ONION FRITTERS

Makes 16

1 lb (450g) plain flour
1 tbsp salt
1 tsp granulated sugar
3 tbsp corn oil
2 tbsp water

10 spring onions,
 chopped very finely
2oz (50g) pork fat
3oz (75g) sesame
 seeds
corn oil for deep-frying

Combine flour, salt and sugar in a bowl;
stir in oil and water. Knead until it forms
a ball. Transfer to a floured surface and
knead until smooth. Roll dough into a long
sausage and cut into 16 portions. Roll each
portion into a round ball. Transfer to a
plastic bag to prevent drying.

Take out 1 ball at a time and roll into a
paper-thin pancake. Place 2 tsp of spring
onions in the centre. Rub pork fat around
sides, then roll pancake into a long sausage.
Pinch both ends to seal. Coil to give a round
fritter and even off with a rolling pin. Repeat
with remaining dough and filling.

Moisten both sides of fritters
with water and press onto sesame
seeds, coating both sides. Dry
off on kitchen paper. Cover base
of a frying pan with ½" (1cm)
oil and bring up to a medium heat.

Pan-fry fritters until golden
brown, 3–4 minutes. Drain on
kitchen paper and serve hot.

DRY-BRAISED BAMBOO SHOOTS

Serves 12–15

1½lb (700g) canned
   bamboo shoots
1½–2 tbsp sweet chilli
   sauce

1½–2 tbsp light soy
½ tsp soft brown sugar
vegetable oil for deep-
   frying
2–3 tsp shaosing wine
   or dry sherry

S lice bamboo shoots into wedges. Blanch
in boiling water for 1 minute. Drain,
refresh in cold water and pat dry with
kitchen paper.

Mix chilli sauce, soy and sugar in a bowl
and put aside.

Heat a wok half-full with oil; when the
temperature reaches 190°C/375°F, add
bamboo shoots. Fry until their edges turn
light brown, about 2 minutes. Remove and
drain on kitchen paper.

Pour off all but 1 tbsp oil from the wok,
return bamboo shoots and stir-fry over a high
heat for 1–2 minutes. Add chilli sauce
mixture and splash in wine and cook for
another 1–2 minutes. Serve immediately and
eat with cocktail sticks.

SZECHUAN SPICY CUCUMBER

Serves 10–15

4 firm cucumbers
2 tbsp salt
4 tbsp soft brown sugar
1 red pepper, deseeded
  and cut into strips
2 tbsp finely chopped
  fresh ginger
4 tbsp sesame oil
4 dried chilli peppers,
  deseeded and
  crushed
1 tsp szechuan pepper
3 tbsp rice wine vinegar
1 tbsp dark soy

C ut each cucumber in half lengthwise;
scoop out and discard soft seeds. Cut
into 1×3″ (2.5×7.5cm) strips. Place in a
bowl mixed with salt and 1 tbsp of sugar, and
leave to stand for 20 minutes.

Rinse cucumber thoroughly and pat dry
with kitchen paper. Transfer to a bowl and
mix with pepper and ginger.

Heat oil in a small pan over low heat and
fry chilli and pepper until golden brown.
Leave to cool for 2 minutes. Then, mix with
vinegar, remaining sugar and soy and pour
over cucumber mixture. Mix well and
refrigerate for 4 hours before serving. Eat
with cocktail sticks.

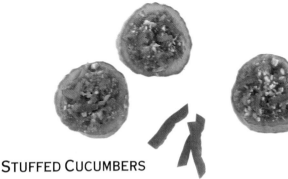

STUFFED CUCUMBERS

Makes 20

4oz (100g) sweet
   potato, quartered
2 large cucumbers
3 dried chinese
   mushrooms,
   reconstituted
2oz (50g) cashew nuts
4oz (100g) canned
   unsweetened
   chestnut purée
10 coriander leaves
1 tbsp light soy
1 tbsp shaosing wine
1 tsp soft brown sugar
seasoning
chopped red pepper for
   garnish

Boil sweet potato for 15 minutes and drain. Peel rind from cucumber and cut into 1" (2.5cm) slices. Using a parisienne cutter or melon baller, carefully scoop out seeds, taking care not to split sides. Finely chop mushrooms, discarding hard stems.

Add sweet potato, mushroom, cashew nuts and chestnut purée to a food processor and process until a coarse paste. Finely chop coriander and add to processor with soy, wine, sugar and seasoning. Blend for 20 seconds.

Generously fill cucumber pieces with stuffing. Arrange, spaced slightly apart, in a steamer and place over a pan of boiling water. Steam in batches for 15 minutes. Remove and drain on kitchen paper for a few minutes. Garnish with red pepper and serve warm.

SMOKED VEGETARIAN DUCK

Makes 20

8oz (225g) dried bean
  curd skins
2 tbsp dark soy
¼pt (150ml) sesame
  oil
1 tsp soft brown sugar
1 tbsp jasmine tea
  leaves
2 tbsp guoba rice
plum sauce for dipping
spring onion rounds for
  garnish

S often bean curd skins in hot water for 5 minutes and drain. Save 3 long pieces and shred remainder finely.

Combine soy and sesame oil in a bowl and add shredded bean curd. Lay out one of bean curd skins and spread with about a third of shredded soy mixture. Roll up skin into a cylinder and repeat with other two skins.

Preheat oven to 180°C/350°F/Gas 4. Place rolls join-side down on a roasting rack and stand in a roasting tray containing brown sugar, tea and guoba rice. Cook for 30 minutes.

Remove rolls (discard rice), leave to cool slightly and then slice carefully. Garnish with spring onion and serve warm on a platter with plum sauce for dipping.

BRAISED CHINESE MUSHROOMS

Makes 15–20

4oz (100g) thin mixed-
  size dried chinese
  mushrooms,
  reconstituted
2 tbsp groundnut or
  vegetable oil
1 tbsp ginger juice
1 tsp soft brown sugar
2½ tbsp dark soy
1½–2 tsp sesame oil

Drain mushrooms, reserving soaking liquid. Leave them damp and halve the very large ones.

Heat a wok over high heat until smoke rises. Add oil and mushrooms and stir for 20–30 seconds. Add ginger juice and sugar and stir rapidly for a few seconds, then add soy and 4–5 fl oz (100–150ml) of mushroom liquid.

Bring to the boil, reduce heat and continue to cook, covered, for about 15 minutes until the liquid has been absorbed. The mushrooms should be very tender by now. If any excess liquid remains, turn up heat to reduce it. Brush with sesame oil and serve warm or cold.

SEAWEED

Serves 10

1lb (450g) fresh
  spinach, washed
corn oil for deep-frying
¼ tsp salt
2 tsp caster sugar

Remove tough stalks from spinach and lay leaves on a large tray to dry. Place 6 or 7 leaves on top of each other and fold into a neat roll; using a sharp knife, slice crosswise to form thin thread-like strips.

Add oil to a wok and heat to 200°C/400°F. Deep-fry spinach strips for about 2 minutes until crisp. Remove with a slotted spoon and drain on kitchen paper.

Leave to cool and transfer to a serving dish. Sprinkle with salt and mix thoroughly; then sprinkle with sugar and mix again. Serve cold.

SPRING ONION SAVOURY

Makes 48

1 ½pt (875ml) corn oil
8oz (225g) spring
  onions, finely chopped
6oz (175g) spanish
  onion, finely chopped
salt and white pepper

PASTRY
8oz (225g) plain flour,
  plus extra for dusting
⅛ tsp salt
4 tbsp melted lard
8 tbsp boiling water

Add half oil to a small pan and sauté
onion for 2 minutes. Transfer to a bowl
and add uncooked spring onion and salt and
pepper. Put to one side.

Make the pastry: sift flour into a large
mixing bowl with salt. Pour in hot melted
lard and boiling water, allowing to cool for a
few seconds first, then mix to a springy
dough. Knead only 3 or 4 times and divide
into 4. Keep moist under a damp cloth.

Sprinkle a work surface with flour and
roll one dough piece into a rectangular
shape. Fold into thirds and roll again. Repeat
3 more times, but the last time roll into a
square. Cut into 4×6 ″ (18cm) squares with
a knife. Place 2 tsp of onion mixture in the
centre of each square, and lift the corners
and fold them diagonally into the centre to
cover. Seal by scalloping the edges. Repeat
with remaining dough to make 16 parcels.

Heat remaining oil in a wok to 180°C/
350°F and deep-fry parcels for 2–3 minutes
until golden. Slice each parcel into 3.

DEEP-FRIED STUFFED MUSHROOMS

Makes 36

13oz (375g) peeled
  shrimps, thawed if
  frozen
1/2 tsp salt
36 medium
  mushrooms, wiped
  and stalks removed
36 coriander leaves
3oz (75g) plain flour
2oz (50g) cornflour,
  plus extra for dusting
6floz (475ml) water
vegetable oil for deep-
  frying
light soy for dipping

Purée shrimps in a blender and add salt.
Sprinkle insides of mushrooms with
cornflour, shaking out any excess. Stuff with
shrimp mixture and press a coriander leaf in
the end.

Mix flour with cornflour in a bowl and stir
in water. Whisk lightly to a batter.

Heat oil in a heavy frying pan to
180°C/350°F. Coat mushrooms in batter and
fry in batches for 2 minutes or until golden.
Drain on kitchen paper. Serve hot with a
bowl of soy sauce as a dip.

DRUNKEN MUSHROOMS

Serves 10

1 lb (450g) button
mushrooms
6 spring onions, finely
chopped
4 cloves garlic, lightly
crushed

2 tbsp finely chopped
fresh ginger
1/4pt (150ml) chicken
stock
6 tbsp shaosing wine or
dry sherry
2 tbsp fresh lemon juice
1 tsp salt

P lace all ingredients in a medium pan
and bring to the boil. Simmer for
10 minutes. Cool and serve at room
temperature or chilled. Eat with
cocktail sticks.

STUFFED CABBAGE PARCELS

Makes 30

1 chinese cabbage
1 1/2 tbsp black
  sweetened vinegar
1 tbsp finely chopped
  fresh ginger

FILLING
1 1/2lb (700g) pork
  steak, minced
2 tbsp minced spring
  onions
1 tbsp minced fresh
  ginger
1 tbsp minced garlic

2 1/2 tbsp light soy
2 tbsp shaosing wine or
  dry sherry
1 tbsp sesame oil
1/4 tsp black pepper
1 tbsp cornflour

BROTH
8floz (225ml) chicken
  stock
2 1/2 tbsp shaosing wine
  or dry sherry
1 1/2 tbsp light soy
1 tsp soft brown sugar
1 tsp cornflour

Separate cabbage leaves from the head and plunge them into a pan of boiling water for 1 minute. Refresh in cold water and set aside.

Mix meat with remaining filling ingredients. Place 2 tsp of mixture in the centre of each cabbage leaf. Roll the leaf edges into the centres to form rectangular parcels. Place join-side down in a casserole.

Mix broth ingredients together and pour over cabbage parcels. Partially cover the dish and cook in a preheated 150°C/300°F/Gas 2 oven for 1 hour. Serve warm in the sauce sprinkled with vinegar and ginger.

SAVOURY CASHEW NUTS

Serves 12–15

1 lb (450g) cashew nuts
vegetable oil for deep-frying
2–3 tsp salt or chinese seasoned salt

Blanch nuts in boiling water for 1 minute, drain in a colander, refresh under cold water and pat dry with kitchen paper.

Half-fill a wok or deep-fryer with oil and add nuts. Place over a high heat and deep-fry nuts until light brown or oil temperature reaches 180–185°C/350–365°F, stirring occasionally.

Remove wok from heat immediately. The nuts will continue to colour in the oil during the next 10 seconds to reach the desired golden brown colour.

Using a large hand strainer, remove nuts from oil and place on a dish lined with greaseproof paper to absorb excess oil. While still hot, sprinkle with spiced salt. Mix well and leave to cool.

PICKLED PEKING CABBAGE

Makes 20

2lb (900g) white
  cabbage, quartered
2 tbsp salt
½–¾" (1–2cm) fresh
  ginger, peeled and
  finely shredded
5 tbsp soft brown sugar
3 tbsp groundnut or
  corn oil
2 tsp sesame oil
3 dried red chillies,
  deseeded and
  chopped
1 tsp szechwan pepper
5 tbsp rice wine vinegar

Shred cabbage as finely as possible. Put in a bowl, mix with salt and leave to stand for 2–3 hours.

Squeeze out excess water from cabbage but leave damp. Transfer to a clean bowl. Place ginger on top of cabbage in the centre. Sprinkle on sugar, taking care not to put it over ginger.

Heat groundnut and sesame oil in a small pan over high heat until smoke rises. Remove from heat and add chilli and pepper. Pour over cabbage, add vinegar and mix well. Leave to stand for 2–3 hours at room temperature before serving.

Egg, Rice & Noodles

A colourful selection of unique tastes
from China, Japan and Indonesia.

Recipes in this chapter include delicacies made from eggs, milk, bean curd, rice and noodles. Unusual but delicious, the food is much more colourful than you might at first imagine, and will pleasantly surprise your party guests. Many of the items are quite economical to make, too, and so make a good addition to your overall selection.

Most of the ingredients are readily available; bean curd and quail's eggs can now be found in most supermarkets and health food stores as well as oriental shops. Drain the curd from its liquid before use. The curd is used in these recipes in fillings and is also made into delicious little tartlet cases – an interesting variation on pastry. The cases can be easily made in bulk and stored in airtight containers until required.

Many other recipes can be made in quantity and brought out of the freezer as and when required. Most can be made at least the day before the party and kept in the refrigerator – in fact, their flavour will often improve. Rice sushi or sushi nigiri are better made in advance, but ensure that they are brought to room temperature before serving. Sushi rolls should be sliced about an hour before serving with a very sharp knife. Aromatic quail's eggs and quail's eggs with tomato and chilli are also good made earlier. One exception to this rule is the deep-fried crispy bean curd, which is best served straight from the pan.

Quail's Eggs with Tomato and Chilli

Makes 24

24 quail's eggs
2 tbsp corn oil
1 tbsp finely chopped garlic
2 tomatoes, skinned, deseeded and very finely chopped
1 tbsp tomato purée
1 tsp sweet chilli sauce
1 tsp shaosing wine or dry sherry
20 coriander leaves, very finely chopped, optional

Bring a small pan of water to the boil. Carefully drop in quail's eggs and boil for 30–40 seconds so that yolks will still be soft. Remove from heat and run under cold water for 5 minutes. Shell carefully.

Heat a wok over a high heat, add oil, then garlic. Stir for 20 seconds then add tomato. Stir-fry for 1 minute and add tomato purée. Add chilli sauce and splash in wine. Wait for sizzling to die down and add peeled eggs; stir the eggs around so that they are coated. Add coriander if using to the wok and stir to coat eggs in green. Remove from wok and serve warm with cocktail sticks.

SPINACH AND PRAWN OMELETTES

Makes 35

*8oz (225g) frozen
    spinach, thawed*
1/2oz (15g) butter
1 tbsp ginger juice
*8oz (225g) raw peeled
    prawns, thawed if
    frozen*
seasoning
4 large eggs
1 tsp salt
vegetable oil for frying

Toss spinach and butter in a pan over high heat for about 3 minutes. Cool then put into a food processor; add ginger juice and process to a purée. Transfer to a bowl.

Put prawns in the processor and chop finely, then add to spinach. Season well.

Break eggs into a bowl, add salt and whisk until frothy. Heat an omelette pan over medium heat with ½ tbsp oil, add about 3 tbsp of egg mixture and make 6–7 omelettes in the usual way, using 3 tbsp egg mixture for each one.

Take 1 omelette and place on a bamboo rolling mat or cloth (the end nearest you should be about 1″ (2.5cm) from the edge of the mat). Thinly spread some spinach and prawn mixture over. Roll up tightly, using the mat to help you. Remove mat and repeat. Cut omelette rolls into 1″ (2.5cm) slices.

CRISPY BEAN CURD PUFFS

Makes 32

4 cakes bean curd
4 tbsp cornflour
1 1/4 tsp seasoned
    salt
vegetable oil for deep-
    frying
seasoned salt for
    dipping
hot chilli sauce for
    dipping, optional

Quarter each bean curd cake, then halve each piece widthways, making 32 cubes altogether. Lay on kitchen paper to absorb excess moisture. In a bowl mix cornflour and spiced salt.

Half-fill a wok or deep-fryer with oil and heat to 190–200°C/375–400°F.

Coat bean curd pieces in cornflour and salt mixture and then deep-fry in batches until pale golden, skins crisp but insides soft and curd-like. Remove with a slotted spoon and drain on kitchen paper.

Place a saucer of spiced salt and one of hot chilli sauce if liked in the centre of a large serving platter, and arrange pieces of bean curd around them. Serve hot.

RICE SUSHI

Makes 36

3 eggs
1 tbsp corn oil
5oz (150g) fresh tuna
6 sheets nori seaweed
rice wine vinegar for
    wetting
1¼lb (550g) sushi
    nigiri (p.137)

4oz (100g) cooked
    spinach, thawed if
    frozen (or 1½lb/
    700g fresh weight,
    cooked)
2oz (50g) pickled red
    ginger, thinly
    shredded

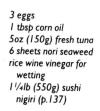

B eat eggs in a bowl until foamy. Heat an omelette pan over medium heat with oil, add eggs and cook for about 1 minute until underside of omelette is light brown. Turn and cook for a further 30 seconds, then remove from pan. Cut into strips and set aside.

Slice tuna into thin ¼×3″ (5mm× 7.5cm) strips. Divide all remaining ingredients into 4.

Lay 1 sheet nori on a bamboo rolling mat. Wet your hand with vinegar. Pat ¼ of rice evenly over nori, leaving a ½″ (1cm) border. Arrange ¼ of spinach, tuna, egg and ginger in strips over rice. Roll up nori using bamboo mat, and press lightly but firmly to produce a neat cylinder. Repeat with remaining ingredients to make up 4 rolls.

Chill rolls for 1 hour, then slice each with a very sharp knife into 9 pieces. Serve at room temperature.

DEEP-FRIED MILK

Makes 30

4oz (100g) solid
 creamed coconut
1½ tsp salt
½ tsp black pepper
5 tbsp cornflour
1pt (575ml) milk

BATTER
6oz (175g) plain flour
5 tbsp cornflour
2 tsp baking powder
½pt (300ml) water
1 tbsp corn oil
corn oil for deep-frying

Grate creamed coconut and put in a pan.
Add salt and pepper. Stir in cornflour.
Stir in some of milk and blend to a smooth
paste, then gradually add remaining milk
over medium heat. Do not boil. Pour into a
shallow baking tray or square casserole
dish and leave to set in the refrigerator for
2 hours.

Make batter: combine plain flour and
cornflour in a bowl, add baking powder; then
gradually stir in water and then oil.

Take mixture from the refrigerator and
cut into 30 diamond pieces. Place a wok over
high heat, add oil and heat to 180°C/350°F.
Dip diamonds lightly into batter and then
carefully drop into the wok. Deep-fry in
batches for about 1 minute until light golden.
Drain on kitchen paper and serve hot.

STUFFED RICE BALLS

Makes 30

10oz (275g) short-
  grain rice, rinsed
1pt (575ml) water
2 tsp salt
4oz (100g) salmon
  steak
½ sheet nori, cut into
  short thin strips
light soy mixed with
  equal part water for
  dipping

Bring rice and water to the boil in a pan over high heat. Cover and simmer for 5 minutes, then reduce heat to as low as possible and cook for 10–15 minutes. Remove from heat and leave to cool, still covered.

Meanwhile, lightly salt salmon and grill under medium heat for 3 minutes on each side. Flake into tiny pieces, removing skin and any bones. Toast nori strips for a few seconds under a high grill and set aside.

Check that rice is cool enough to handle. Take a tsp of rice and flatten it between the palms of your hands. Take about a tsp of salmon and force it into the centre of the flattened rice cake. Roll firmly into small balls. Take several nori strips and press them around the balls. Serve with light soy dip.

Soy Sauce Bean Curd

Makes 64

2 cakes bean curd
4 tbsp corn oil
6 spring onions, sliced

SAUCE
1/4 tsp salt
1/4 tsp soft brown sugar
2 tsp oyster sauce
1 tbsp light soy
1 tsp shaosing wine or
    dry sherry

Soak bean curd in hot water for 15 minutes, then cut each cake into 32 cubes (quarter each cake, then quarter each quarter and cut each piece in half). Drain in a sieve.

Mix all sauce ingredients together in a bowl and put to one side.

Heat oil in a wok over high heat. Add spring onion and bean curd cubes, and stir-fry very gently for 1 minute. Add sauce, lower heat and cook for a further minute. Serve immediately. Eat with cocktail sticks.

AROMATIC QUAIL'S EGGS

Makes 48

2 tbsp jasmine tea
  leaves
48 quail's eggs, boiled
  over low heat for
  45–60 seconds
1pt (575ml) water
1½ tsp salt
2 tbsp light soy
2 tsp soft brown sugar
1½ whole or 12
  segments star anise
1½" (4cm) cinnamon
  stick

Boil tea leaves in the water for 5 minutes to extract their essence. Strain tea and discard leaves.

Gently crack eggs by applying pressure with your palm and rolling eggs one by one on a table, to give a network of fine cracks on each shell.

Put all eggs in a pan large enough to hold them in a single layer. Pour in tea, and add salt, soy, sugar, star anise and cinnamon. If the liquid is not sufficient to cover the eggs, add some water. Gently bring to the boil, reduce heat and simmer, covered, for 20–25 minutes.

Remove from heat and leave eggs in liquid for about 6 hours or overnight, to allow the liquid which has seeped through the cracks to season the eggs. Shortly before serving, remove eggs from liquid and peel off shells. Serve cold or at room temperature.

HUNDRED-YEAR-OLD EGGS

Makes 24

6 lime-cured eggs
3 tsp finely grated fresh
  ginger
1/8 cucumber, sliced
  and cut into tiny
  batons
24 cocktail sticks
24 small pieces
  preserved stem
  ginger, cut into thin
  slices

Shell and quarter each egg. Sprinkle fresh ginger over each quarter. Garnish with cucumber batons and then skewer each quarter with a cocktail stick and a slice of preserved ginger.

INDONESIAN STUFFED EGGS

Makes 20

10 eggs
3oz (75g) ghee
½ spanish onion, very
  finely chopped
2 dried chillies, very
  finely diced
3 cloves garlic, very
  finely chopped
2 sticks celery, very
  finely chopped
1½ tsp shrimp paste
black pepper to taste
1oz (25g) roasted
  peanuts, finely
  crunched
⅛ red pepper, cut
  into tiny slithers

Hard-boil eggs and shell when cool. Place a small pan over medium heat and add ghee. Then add onion, chilli, garlic and celery. Sauté for 3 minutes until onion is opaque but not brown. Add shrimp paste and stir in well. Add black pepper to taste. Remove from heat.

Cut each egg in half and remove yolks. Force yolks through a sieve into the pan containing onion mixture. Combine with a fork.

Fill each egg half with mixture, using a piping bag and wide nozzle or a teaspoon dipped in hot water after filling each half. Sprinkle with finely crunched peanuts and red pepper slithers and serve cold.

SUSHI NIGIRI

Makes 30

1 1/4 lb (550g) medium-
  grain rice
1 1/4 pt (725ml) water
3 1/2 floz (90ml) rice
  wine vinegar
4 tbsp soft brown sugar
2 tsp salt
1 pkt salt-preserved
  ginger (beni-shoga),
  thinly shredded
2 tsp anise seeds
thin shreds green and
  white spring onion

W ash rice thoroughly in cold water.
Transfer to a pan and cover with the
water. Leave for 1 hour. Then, place a lid on
the pan, bring to the boil and simmer for 15
minutes. Do not remove lid. Turn off heat
and leave rice to stand for 10 minutes.

Mix vinegar, sugar and salt in a pan over
medium heat. Heat until sugar is dissolved,
about 2 minutes.

Fluff up rice with a fork, pour over hot
liquid and toss lightly. Take a tbsp of rice
and press into a small ball with your fingers;
repeat until all rice is used. Top each with
beni-shoga, anise seeds and onion strips.
Serve cold.

Sweets & Sweetmeats

Unusual and succulent, oriental
sweets that round off your palate
and the party.

T he oriental dessert, unlike its Western
counterpart, does not contain much
dairy produce. It does however contain large
concentrations of sugar – sugar is regarded
as a luxury item in the Far East and for this
reason highly sweet things are considered
very special.

You may or may not wish to include sweet
recipes among the savoury for a drinks party
– perhaps if the occasion is to be a long one,
the menu could be more extensive and
include some. The recipes in this chapter
may provide a welcome change at the end of
the evening. They would also make good
sweetmeats for the end of a dinner party.

Some items can easily be made in
advance of the party, such as mango jellies
or sweet bean and pine nut tofu. Deep-fried
recipes may be rather too complicated to
make in quantity at the last minute, but are
popular. Best of all are the caramelised
bananas – use a sugar thermometer if
possible, and take care when handling the
caramel.

SPICY FRUIT SALAD

Serves 20

1 apple
1 pear
1 mango, slightly
   under-ripe
½ tsp salt
1 grapefruit
1 lb (500g) can lychees
20 seedless grapes
1 tsp tamarind sauce
3oz (75g) soft brown
   sugar
pinch chilli powder

Peel apple, pear and mango and cut into bite-size pieces. Place all peeled fruit in a bowl and cover with cold water. Add salt. Peel grapefruit, remove pith and divide into segments. Drain lychees, retaining the juice.

Drain other fruit and place all in a shallow serving dish. Combine tamarind with sugar, chilli powder and lychee juice. Pour over fruit and serve with cocktail sticks.

SWEET MOON CAKES

Makes 24

FILLING
2oz (50g) chopped
  dates
3oz (75g) dried
  apricots, soaked
3oz (75g) flaked
  coconut
3oz (75g) raisins
3oz (75g) walnuts,
  coarsely chopped

DOUGH
1lb (450g) plain flour
1 tbsp baking powder
1 tsp salt
3 eggs
3oz (75g) caster sugar
3oz (75g) unsalted
  butter, melted
1 tsp vanilla essence
2 tbsp water
1 egg, lightly beaten

Mix all filling ingredients in a bowl.
Divide into 24 portions.

For dough: sift flour, baking powder and
salt into a bowl . In another bowl, beat eggs
and sugar for 10 minutes. Add melted butter,
vanilla, water and flour mixture. Stir until a
rough dough is formed. Roll the dough into a
long sausage, 1¼" (3cm) thick. Slice into 24.

Press each dough slice into a 3" (7.5cm)
circle and place filling in the centre. Pull
edges to centre and pinch to seal. Roll into a
ball and press into a 1" (2.5cm) circular
baking mould to shape it. Turn cake out and
repeat for all dough slices.

Arrange cakes on a baking sheet 1"
(2.5cm) apart. Mix egg and a little water for
glaze together and brush over cakes. Bake in
a preheated 180°C/350°F/Gas 4 oven for ½
hour until golden brown. Serve warm.

SWEET RICE BALLS

Makes 20

6oz (175g) sesame
  seeds
1 tbsp unsalted butter,
  softened
3oz (75g) soft brown
  sugar
6oz (175g) sweet rice
  flour
1 tbsp corn oil
7floz (200ml) boiling
  water

SYRUP
1/2pt (300ml) water
4oz (100g) caster
  sugar
1" (2.5cm) fresh ginger,
  peeled and crushed

Toast sesame seeds under a medium grill
for 1–2 minutes. Process in a blender.
Add butter and sugar, and process again for
30 seconds. Turn mixture onto a board and
knead lightly to bring together. Roll into a
long sausage and cut into 20 pieces.

Mix rice flour with oil and boiling water
in a bowl to form a rough dough. Roll as
before and cut into 20 pieces. Flatten each
piece of dough to a 3" (7.5cm) circle. Place
sesame paste piece in the centre of each,
pull up the edges and pinch to seal. Roll to
form a ball.

Put water, sugar and ginger in a pan,
bring to boil and simmer for 15 minutes.
Add rice balls and simmer for 8 minutes or
until they float to the surface. Serve
immediately. Eat with cocktail sticks.

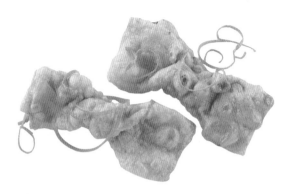

SWEET DEEP-FRIED WONTONS

Makes 12

11oz (300g) dates,
  finely chopped
4oz (100g) walnuts,
  finely chopped
grated rind ¼ orange
2 tbsp fresh orange
  juice
12 wonton wrappers
corn oil for deep-frying
orange zest strips for
  garnish

Mix dates and walnuts in a bowl with orange rind and juice. Place a tsp of this mixture onto each wonton paper. Fold the paper over, moistening edges with water, and twist both ends to seal.

Heat oil in a wok to 170°C/325°F and deep-fry wontons until golden brown. Drain on kitchen paper and garnish with zest. Serve hot.

COCONUT RICE CAKE

Makes 30

1 lb (450g) glutinous
  rice, soaked for 4–6
  hours
1 ½ pt (875ml) water
4 tbsp sweetened
  desiccated coconut
1 ½ tbsp anise seeds
6 tbsp caster sugar
3 tbsp melted butter
a little vegetable oil
anise seeds for garnish,
  optional

Put rice in a pan with the water, cover and cook over a medium heat – this will take about 10 minutes. Remove from heat and leave to stand for another 15 minutes. Do not remove the lid in this time. Then, fluff up rice with a fork.

While cooked rice is still hot, stir in the coconut, anise, sugar and butter. Mix well.

Brush an 8–10″ (20–30cm) baking tray with a little vegetable oil and pack in rice mixture tightly, forming an even surface. Refrigerate for ½ hour and cut into 30 small squares when ready to serve. Sprinkle over extra anise seeds if liked. Serve cold.

SWEET BEAN AND PINE NUT TOFU

Makes 16

4 cakes bean curd
corn oil for deep-frying

3floz (75g) sweet black
bean paste
48 pine nuts

Drain bean curd, remove surface skin and pat dry kitchen paper. Quarter each to make 16 squares.

Heat oil in a wok to 140°C/275°F. Deep-fry bean curd squares for 6–7 minutes until golden. Drain on kitchen paper and leave to cool.

Cut a square in the top of each curd piece and hollow out the centre. Fill with bean paste and top with pine nuts. Bake in a preheated 200°C/400°F/Gas 6 oven for 6 minutes. Serve hot.

SWEET CASHEW NUTS

Serves 10

1 lb (450g) cashew nuts
¾pt (450ml) water
8oz (225g) caster
   sugar
2 tsp sesame seeds
corn oil for deep-frying

Blanch nuts in boiling water for 1 minute
and drain.

Put water and sugar in a pan and cook
over a low heat until sugar is dissolved. Add
nuts and simmer for 4 minutes. Remove from
heat and leave to soak for 2 hours. Drain
completely.

Toast sesame seeds under a medium grill
for 1–2 minutes. Heat oil in a pan to
180°C/350°F and deep-fry nuts for 2 minutes.
Drain on kitchen paper and sprinkle with
sesame seeds.

CARAMELISED BANANAS

Makes 48

corn oil for deep-frying
6 large bananas
2 tbsp plain flour
6 tbsp groundnut oil
12 tbsp soft brown
    sugar
2 tsp sesame seeds

BATTER
7oz (200g) self-raising
    flour
2 eggs, lightly beaten
9floz (250ml) water
2 tbsp corn oil

Make batter: Mix flour and egg in a bowl, and gradually add water. Leave to stand for 15 minutes then blend in oil.

Heat corn oil in a wok to 180°C/350°F. Cut each banana into 8 pieces and toss them in plain flour. Dip banana in batter and deep-fry for 2–3 minutes until light golden. Drain on kitchen paper and set aside.

Fill a large bowl with iced water. Heat groundnut oil in a fresh pan. When hot, add sugar. Let it dissolve over medium heat, stirring all the time. When it turns light brown add all the banana pieces and sesame seeds. Stir to coat the bananas with syrup and sesame seeds. Remove and dip in iced water, and serve immediately.

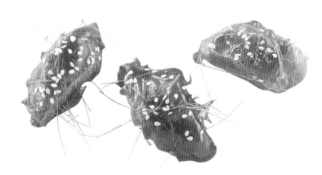

MANGO JELLIES

Makes 30

½oz (15g) agar-agar
½pt (300ml) warm
  water
2pt (1.5ltr) cold water
6oz (175g) soft brown
  sugar
3floz (75ml)
  evaporated milk
2×1lb (500g) cans
  mangoes, drained and
  finely chopped

Soak agar-agar in warm water for ½ hour. Transfer to a pan and add cold water. Cook over medium heat until agar is completely dissolved, 3–4 minutes. Remove from heat. Add sugar, milk and mango, and stir until sugar is dissolved. Pour into 2 8×12″ (20×30cm) lightly greased cake tins. Refrigerate until firm, then cut into diamond shapes.

Red Bean Pancakes

Makes 12

1 egg, lightly beaten
5 tbsp plain flour
4 tbsp water
4 tbsp red bean paste
beaten egg for sealing
corn oil for deep-frying

Mix egg and flour together in a bowl. Stir in the water slowly to form a batter. Leave to stand for 40 minutes. Divide into 2 portions.

Cook 2 large pancakes, 1 at a time, in an oiled frying pan for 2 minutes. Do not turn over. Remove from the pan and place on a flat surface. Spread 2 tbsp of bean paste along the centre of each pancake. Fold to form 2 rectangular parcels. Seal the edges with beaten egg.

Heat oil in a wok to 180°C/350°F and deep-fry parcels for 3–4 minutes until golden. Drain on kitchen paper. Cut each parcel widthways at an angle to make 6 strips. Serve immediately.

SWEET WALNUT SQUARES

Makes 90

4oz (100g) walnuts,
    crushed
4oz (100g) sweet black
    bean paste
flour and water for
    sticking
corn oil for deep-frying
icing sugar for dusting

BATTER
12oz (350g) plain flour
pinch salt
4 eggs, beaten
1pt (575ml) milk

Make batter: sift flour and salt into a
bowl. Mix in eggs and gradually add
milk. Chill mixture for ½ hour before making
30 small, thin pancakes in the usual way.

Take a small square cutter and cut out as
many shapes as possible from pancakes. Set
aside in pairs.

Mix walnuts with black bean paste. Put
½ tsp in the centre of one square, and
sandwich with the other. Seal edges with a
little flour and water paste. Repeat until all
squares and filling are used.

Heat oil in a wok to 140°C/275°F and
deep-fry squares until golden. Drain on
kitchen paper. Dust with icing sugar.

MANDARIN PANCAKES

Makes 24

10oz (275g) plain flour
¼ tsp salt
4floz (100ml) boiling
  water

1 tbsp corn oil
plain flour for dusting
5 tbsp sesame oil

Sift flour with salt into a bowl. Add boiling water, then corn oil. Mix well to form a dough. Remove from bowl to a flat, floured surface and knead lightly for 5–10 minutes until bouncy. Divide into 4 equal pieces and form a cylindrical roll with each piece. Slice each roll into 6 pieces.

Flatten each dough ball between the palms of your hands to form a 2″ (5cm) circle. Brush one circle with a little sesame oil and place another circle (not brushed with oil) on top. Repeat to make 12 pairs of dough circles. Roll out dual-dough circles to form 12 thin pancakes about 5–6″ (12–15cm) wide.

Fry each pancake in an omelette pan without oil for 1–2 minutes, turning once. Small brown patches should appear on the surface of the pancakes. Remove and cool. Peel apart to form 2 thin pancakes. Repeat and store between layers of greaseproof paper in a sealed container ready for use. Freeze if liked in batches of 12 between greaseproof layers in a polythene bag.

FILO TARTLETS

Makes 32

8 sheets filo pastry
corn oil for brushing
32 tartlet moulds or
cases

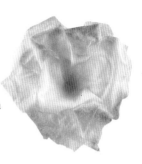

Cut filo into squares of approx. 2″ (5cm). Brush each filo square lightly with oil and, using the pastry brush, gently push each sheet into a tartlet mould so that it loosely lines the sides. Use 4 sheets per case – it is best if they line the case unevenly.

Bake in a preheated 150°C/300°F/Gas 2 oven for 10–15 minutes until light golden. Remove and store carefully.

CRISPY BEAN CURD CASES

Makes 64

4 cakes bean curd
corn oil for deep-frying

Quarter each cake of bean curd, then halve each quarter. Drain thoroughly on kitchen paper.

Add oil to a wok and heat to 190°C/375°F. Add one quarter of bean curd pieces to oil and deep-fry for 10–15 minutes until golden brown. Remove and drain on kitchen paper; repeat with remainder.

When required for use, slice each case in half and scoop out any centre remaining. Serve warm or cold.

oyster sauce

sweet chilli sauce

wasabi paste

sweetened black
vinegar

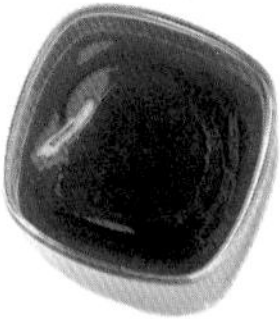

hoisin sauce

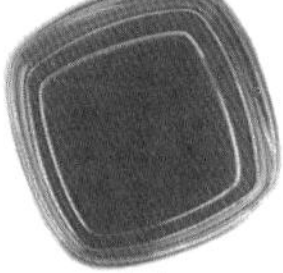

mirin

black mushrooms

dried shrimps

yellow bean sauce

star anise
with 5-spice powder

szechuan pepper

cashew nuts

guoba rice

miso

dried chinese mushrooms

fermented black beans

black sesame seeds

water chestnuts

dried lime peel

pickled ginger slices

fresh ginger slices

nori

red bean paste

chinese seasoned salt